Prices and Production

Albrecht Ritschl

Prices and Production

Elements of a System-Theoretic Perspective

With 28 Figures

Physica-Verlag Heidelberg

Series Editor

Werner A. Müller

Author

Dr. Albrecht Ritschl
Department of Economics
University of Munich
Ludwigstrasse 33/IV
D-8000 Munich 22, FRG

ISBN 3-7908-0429-0 Physica-Verlag Heidelberg
ISBN 0-387-91356-4 Springer-Verlag New York

CIP-Titelaufnahme der Deutschen Bibliothek
Ritschl, Albrecht:
Prices and production: elements of a system-theoretic
perspective/Albrecht Ritschl. – Heidelberg: Physica-Verl., 1989
(Contributions to economics; 1)
Zugl.: München, Univ., Diss., 1987
ISBN 3-7908-0429-0
NE: GT

Printing: Weihert-Druck GmbH, Darmstadt
Bookbinding: J. Schäffer GmbH u. Co. KG, Grünstadt
7120/7130-543210

Acknowledgements

This text is the translated and revised version of my doctoral dissertation, presented in 1987 to the Faculty of Economics, University of Munich. Above all, I wish to thank my referees, Professors E. von Böventer and H.-D. Wenzel, for their continuous patience and advice. Deep thanks go also to Professor K. Borchardt, without whose kind concern this book would have been impossible.

Preliminary versions of my work have been presented to the Research Seminar of our Faculty, and I am grateful to its members, esp. Professors H. Möller, H.-W. Sinn, and F. Gehrels, for their most helpful comments and suggestions.

I also had the opportunity to discuss portions of this work with Professor B. Schefold and his staff at the University of Frankfurt. Though I did not follow his advice everywhere, the substantial influence of Professor Schefold's suggestions and his own writings is evident throughout this book. But of course this does not imply that he shares all of my views.

Special thanks as well go to Professor Richard Adelstein of Wesleyan University, Middletown, Connecticut, who kindly read the working translation of the manuscript and seems to have managed to convert my broken English into a readable text.

Financial support from the Bavarian Graduates Promotion Program is also gratefully acknowledged.

Albrecht Ritschl
Munich, Fall 1988

Contents:

0. Introduction

My original intention in writing this book was to consider evolving market systems and Hayekian criteria of efficiency (see von Hayek (1931, 1945)), and to discover those formal structures which might possibly lie at the base of economic systems capable of evolution. Much work in this field had already been done by others (see, for example, Kirzner (1975) and Nelson/Winter (1982)), and a consensus seems to have been reached that something like system theory must be the logical point of departure for evolutionary theory in economics. But most of the previous work in this area is purely intuitive, and though there is much talk in it of systems and system theory, a precise definition of the concept of a system in this context is nowhere to be found. I had hoped to be able to sketch a working definition of pricing and production systems in a few pages and then to go on to investigate their performance within the framework of modern stability analysis. It soon became clear, however, that difficult and complex problems arise from the very outset of such an endeavor. If, for example, one speaks of dynamic systems of pricing and production, it should be made clear just how these systems differ from those portrayed in standard price theory and why that theory is inadequate for such analysis. Because the existing literature in evolutionary economics offers no clear answers to these questions, economists accustomed to thinking of preferences and scarcities as the primary determinants of price formation might justifiably ask what the real advantage of all this new theoretical apparatus is.

But to examine these problems meant changing the direction of the present research itself. Instead of considering the potential problems of stability in complex economic systems, we shall concentrate here on the more basic task of developing the analysis of price and production systems along the lines of linear system theory. Once this has been done, we can proceed to our principal question, the relationship between systems of this kind and the more standard models of microeconomic theory.

We begin with what appears to be the most important consideration for "nonstandard" theorizing in the area of pricing, the element of time in production. As von Hayek's classic 1931 study *Prices and Production* makes clear, there is nothing new about the incorporation of time into the analysis of production. But the teachings of books such as this have scarcely penetrated the corpus of modern theory at all; contemporary economists seem instead to be educated in a tradition which suggests that time generally makes no difference in production, and where it does, its effects can readily be introduced by way of simple side restrictions. Still, some modern price theorists, such as Sir John Hicks (1973), have argued that this traditional intuition is

1

incorrect and misleading, and the book which follows represents an attempt to explore the implications of this argument more further.

Economic production is, among other things, a material flow from nature to a sphere of production and back again. Because this material flow takes time and consumes energy, it is natural to conceive of production as an open system, and if this is indeed the case, the theoretical apparatus developed for the analysis of open systems in other areas should find application here as well. After two decades of debate regarding the environmental consequences of modern, large–scale production, this general perspective should hardly seem new or surprising. But it was a radical departure indeed when first suggested by Georgescu–Roegen (1966, 1971), and to this day has not found general acceptance in the discipline of economics. The formal description of this material flow, at least in its basic form, is clearly not a problem of pure economic theory alone. More specifically, the economist is not entirely free to choose the way in which such a system can be investigated, for the models he employs are bound by certain natural constraints whose roots lie in the basic principles of physics. It cannot, for example, be possible to produce something from nothing, nor can there be `perpetuum mobile` or velocities of infinite magnitude[1]. System theory is a highly general approach to the analysis of such problems in a consistent way. It thus seems reasonable first to construct a system– theoretic model of prices and production and then to evaluate existing economic systems on the basis of this model. In doing so, we shall in fact employ a most useful criterion of consistency introduced by Frisch (1935; see also Samuelson (1947)), to the effect that a static economic model, if it is to be consistent, must be the limiting case (that is, the stationary state) of an underlying dynamic model. We shall adopt this standard as a measure of the consistency of economic analysis conducted from a system–theoretic perspective.

Production, like price formation, takes time. Theorists have long understood that in the course of "capitalist" production all processes must be financed before they are begun. To Böhm–Bawerk (1889), a production process is capitalistic if it requires intermediate products, for the production of these intermediates demands time, during which the means of life must be provided from stocks already accumulated. If people discount future earnings by positive rates of interest, production processes which take time will

---

[1] These constraints have been discussed in the context of economic Activity Analysis, see the volume edited by Koopmans (1951). From a technical point of view, activity analysis is just a reformulation of von Neumann's system of growth and will therefore not be dealt with explicitly. See Hausman (1981) for a comparison of value theories from the viewpoint of activity analysis.

be undertaken only if their return over the value of the inputs is at least as great as the rate of interest. Stated in terms of prices, this means that there is always an interest factor which intervenes between input prices and output prices in the process of production, an observation which will be the focal point of the analysis which follows.

The economic problem proper is introduced when we move from physical systems dealing with quantities to price systems. Economic theory, whatever shcool of thought it might be drawn from, generally maintains that the system of commodity production is steered in some way or another by the price system. This is plainly a duality argument regarding system controllability, and we shall examine in what way price systems are dual to quantity systems. None of this, of course, is a journey through no man's land. There is, above all, von Neumann's (1937) famous dynamic system with a dual price system, and much of this book can usefully be seen as a review of generalizations of his model. But there is a class of economic models, the systems of equilibrium based on the theory of Walras (1874), which do not fit into this framework, and we shall argue that these models are inconsistent when regarded from a system–theoretic perspective.

Much of price theory has been concerned with reducing the problem of economic control through prices to the values of external inputs which are under control of the economic agents. Because there is no generally agreed upon measure of "value", the validity of value theories has been a subject of debate which continues even today. Such external values are employed neither by von Neumann's price system nor by the related system of Sraffa (1960), and it will be argued that if system–theoretic conditions of consistency are applied to production systems, the related price system cannot be expressed in terms of external values without the introduction of bias. Such reasoning is not entirely new to economics, and its manifestation in the Marxist labor theory of value is known as the "Transformation Problem". We shall show that the same transformation problem arises in Walras' theory of value as well, and its general applicability to other possible systems of external values is to be presumed.

Chapter 1 seeks to introduce the general problem on an intuitive level. In Section 1.1., the element of time in production is considered in the context of an example, and as means of illustration we employ what is known in demography as a "Lexis diagram", a scheme which represents the path of age cohorts through time. A three–stage production process is considered and generalized in steps. The same device also proves useful when capital goods are considered, for the stock of durables at any moment in time can be seen as a population of different vintages, and with Lexis' scheme these stocks can be reduced to a sequence of flows.

3

Some of the implications of time in production for the formation of prices are considered as well. In Section 1.2., we argue that all production processes which take time must be financed before they commence, and so in an economy with interest calculation there will in general be interest charges on such capital outlays. Circulating capital which bears interest is thus a characteristic of production–based price systems.

Chapter 2 is the theoretical foundation for further analysis. In Section 2.1., production relations are modeled as state– transition functions of a linear, discrete–time system. It shows that in some cases, this system can be transformed into a difference–equation input–output system, where the latter is the backward–recursive form of the former. Systems capable of such transformation reveal themselves to be basic–commodity systems in the sense of Sraffa (1960). Following Livesey (1973), there has been a discussion of singularity in dynamic economic systems, but with basic–commodity systems, there is no such problem; singular systems will be either non–basic or time–inconsistent or both. In the case of balanced (exponential) growth, there is a strictly positive eigenvector to the basic system. Economic theory usually regards production as a static problem, which is best approached through cross–section analysis of dynamic systems. If such analysis is applied to dynamic production schemes, there are certain biases, and with exponential growth of production, this bias is systematic.

Durable capital goods are introduced in Section 2.1.2. We envision capital goods as a population with as many genders as there are different kinds of such goods. The process of aging is described by patterns of survival probabilities which can be understood as dependent upon prices. This leads to a system of stocks which exists alongside the flow system of commodity production. The interrelationship between these systems is given by a system of stock–input equations, where the flow system supplies the inputs to the stock system. Assuming balanced exponential growth, we introduce a reduced system of flows where all interactions with capital goods are integrated. This system can also be solved using eigenvalue theorems.

Section 2.2. considers price systems, beginning in Section 2.2.1. with an examination of the prices of flows. In principle, commodity prices are determined by the prices of commodity inputs and the prices of external inputs such as labor or rents for the use of natural resources. In a dynamic context, these input prices are weighted not only by their input coefficients but by one–period rates of interest. The resulting system of price equations is that of von Neumann (1937) and Sraffa (1960), and we show that it can be regarded as the dual to the backward–recursive quantity systems of Section 2.1.1., although this duality is somewhat loose. In particular, when constant prices are assumed, the number of combinations of wages and profits which are consistent with a given physical rate of growth is infinite, and vice versa. Assuming an exponential rise or fall of prices (that is, a constant rate of inflation or deflation), we apply a cross–sectional analysis to the price system to show that the estimator of the one–period rate of interest is equal to Fisher's (1930) real rate of interest.

Section 2.2.2. considers price systems with durable capital goods. The problem here lies in the interaction of commodity prices and stock prices; capital goods must be paid their cost of production when first installed, but their price must in some way or another be incorporated into to the prices of the commodities produced by means of these capital stocks. If prices and quantities are stationary or growing exponentially over time, a general solution to this system can be specified. We consider an integrated price system in which the values of all the inputs and outputs ever produced with the services of a given capital good are added together, so that, just as in the system of Sraffa (1960), both user costs and prices of used equipments can be determined from commodity prices. In Section 2.2.3., prices of joint products are considered briefly. In capital theory, there seems to be general agreement that only with joint–production systems can the formation prices of durable capital goods be adequately explained, but in Chapter 3, it is shown that in fact this approach and that of Section 2.2. are equivalent.

Sec. 2.3. is an effort to generalize some of the results of the analysis to this point. First, we consider generalized input–output patterns in which the flow of output at a given time is the result of a sequence of lagged inputs. Under steady–state conditions, or with time–invariant techniques, such sequences can be readily mapped into an input–output matrix with a uniform one–period lag. With time–dependent matrices, no such well–defined relation exists, so the behavior of the system cannot be predicted from its one–period state transitions. A second issue is raised by the transition from discrete time to continuous time. The conventional wisdom is that intermediate products must be defined so as to render all production steps of equal length. In the limit, as the production period approaches zero, this leads to an infinitely large number of commoditites. We show that, contrary to this conventional result, the number of commodities can be held constant. But the matrices which relate these commodities to one another must now be interpreted with care, and they are still not independent of the time scale of the underlying discrete–time system. We then include inventories in our analysis. Insofar as most price–theoretic models implicitly assume (rather than prove) that markets always clear, inventories are simply assumed away. Without investigating this issue in great depth, we examine flow systems with inventories and derive some steady–state conditions. Finally, the problem of system controllability is considered. We show that at least with regard to the

5

quantity systems we analyze in Section 2.1., systems of basic commodities in Sraffa's sense have the property of both complete controllability and complete observability.

Chapter 3 considers existing economic theories in light of our own theoretical results. In Section 3.1., prominent models which either assume that economic activity requires no time at all or employ a rather ambiguous concept of preiodicity in which the period length is in fact is equal to zero are reviewed. Such models produce certain biases when applied to dynamic production structures. Where quantities are concerned, they depict the underlying dynamic systems incorrectly in all but the stationary state of no growth. Their price equations, moreover, neglect interest charges on circulating capital because no period of production is assumed, and are thus valid only in an economy in which interest charges are zero. We begin in Section 3.1.1. with the so-called dynamic system of Leontief (1953), which has been the target of criticism of system theory. We show that its inconsistency is due to ambiguous assumptions regarding time intervals, and although it is possible to remove its inherent contradictions, the explanatory power of the system which results is substantially reduced.

In Section 3.1.2., the same reasoning is applied to the system of Walras (1874) which remains today the centerpiece of value theory. Walras himself explicitly excluded time from his analysis, and we argue here that when time is introduced to his system, the results wich are produced are devoid of meaning. This claim is not a new one; it seems to have been common to the Austrian School, and some modern writers, such as Shackle (1958), have raised the issue as well. It appears that, contrary to Walras'conclusions, to the extent that interest charges drive a wedge between values and prices, prices cannot all be reduced to scarcity values. We turn in Section 3.1.3. to production functions in one-commodity settings. Though their "timeless" versions show similar biases, there is no problem with introducing production lags in this case, for theory of this case implicitly assumes a one-stage production process. We thus extend the analysis to the example of a two-stage proceess of production in which the output of the first¯stage enters into the process of the second stage. We show that the attempt construct an aggregate production function must fail even in this simple case, for the rate of substitution between capital in the first and second stages is equal to the interest factor. Thin in turn implies that no capital aggregate exists independently of the rate of interest.

There is also a class of economic models which describe prices and production in a time-consistent way. These are considered in Section 3.2. At the core of modern dynamic theory lies von Neumann's (1937) system of a growing economy. Though usually approached through the techniques of linear optimization, some of the equilibrium properties can be demonstrated using simple matrix algebra. A closely related system is that of Sraffa (1960). Modern capital theorists seem to agree that only through his joint–production approach can durable capital goods adequately be treated. In Section 3.2.2., however, we show that the subsystem approach employed in Chapter 2 is equivalent to that of Sraffa.

A classic treatment of a dynamic economic system is that of Marx (1885, 1894). In Section 3.2.3., we first consider his analysis in terms of his own price equations and offer steady–state solutions to his model of extended reproduction. These equations are then translated into our input–output framework, where equivalent conditions can be specified. Durable capital goods are included without resort to the joint–production approach. A lengthy controversy regarding technical progress and secular tendencies in the rate of profit has followed in the wake of Samuelson (1957) and Okishio (1963), and we derive here conditions of Harrod–neutral progress under which the organic composition of capital remains unchanged. It is also shown that other forms of progress are necessarily nonneutral and that, as a rule, no clear predicition can be made as to the time path of the rate of profit.

In the concluding section, some general results concerning the phenomenon of value are presented. For many years, various price theories of quite different kinds have sought to find the external variables which control to the price system, that is, values. By exerting control over the price system, which in turn was held to control quantities, values were said to explain the movement of the entire economic system, a chain of reasoning which brought to economics its dubious distinction as the "dismal science". But this is a clear example of system–theoretic reasoning as well. Basic–commodity systems are both observable and controllable, with external inputs as the control variables. Price systems are dual to quantity systems, and if these are controllable by values, then overall economic control through values is well possible.

The critical discussion of the Marxist labor theory value teaches that the prices of commodities are in general not proportional to the values embodied by those commodities, that is, the relative price of two commodity differs from the ratio of their labor values. This, as we have noticed, is the "Transformation Problem". We demonstrate in Section 3.3. that this problem arises in a much wider range of theories, for the bias we find in Walras' price equations reveals itself as equivalent to that of Marxist values, save the scalar of labor inputs in the case of the labor theory is replaced by a vector of resource inputs in the Walrasian case. Only if the ratio of direct to indirect resource inputs is the same for all commodities in the Walrasian system does the transformation problem disappear; the problem of unequal organic com-

7

positions of capital arises in Walras' theory as well as in Marx's. In general, external values seem to be an insufficient basis for the explanation of prices.

This problem of transformation between the values of inputs and the prices of outputs has serious consequences for the controllability of economic activity. Since the rate of interest tends to introduce a bias between input and output prices, the price system cannot be completely controlled by the allocative choice of inputs. This in turn implies that, contrary to the conventional wisdom of economic thought, economic self–control by means of relative prices is necessarily incomplete.

1. Time in the Economic Equations of Prices and Production

1.1. Production Equations

We begin with a simple example which will soon be generalized. Consider time as a sequence of points t_0, t_1, t_2 etc. which follow one another in a given distance which we shall call a time step. All events in the world last for a minimum of one time step, which may be arbitrarily small. Consider first the process of producing a consumption good whose quantity is represented as C. This consumption good is produced in three successive steps, each of which lasts one time step (so that the time step is our elementary period of production). Assume that production in the first stage requires only raw materials taken from nature in quantity R_1 plus human labor in quantity L_1; to produce intermediate outputs in quantity X_1. The product X_1 is then combined with raw materials R_2 and labor L_2 in the second stage of production I_2 to produce new intermediate products X_2. In the final stage of the process, I_3, C units of the consumption good itself are produced by combining X_2 with new inputs of raw materials and labor R_3 and L_3. Employing the symbol $\oplus$ to connote combination in production as determined by the available technology, we may represent this three–stage process as follows (see Bliss (1977)):

$$
\begin{array}{llll}
I_1: & R_1 \oplus L_1 & \longrightarrow & X_1 \\
I_2: & R_2 \oplus L_2 \oplus X_1 & \longrightarrow & X_2 \\
I_3: & R_3 \oplus L_3 \oplus X_2 & \longrightarrow & C
\end{array}
$$

The three stages of production are not independent; not only must they share the supply of labor, but the intermediate stages I_3 and I_2 must rely on the outputs of the preceding stages as well. It is this second interdependence which introduces the element of time. Production in stage I_2 may begin at time t_1 only if positive quantities of intermediate outputs X_1 have been produced in I_1 during the time step just passed, $t_1 - t_0$, and similarly one time step after for stage I_3 and intermediate products X_2. Thus, the path of any given particle of raw material through its different stages of processing can be seen as a path of that input through time. At time t_0, the raw material enters the first stage I_1 where it leaves as unfinished material at time t_1. Transformed once more in the second stage, it passes from I_2 at time t_2, so that at t_3 it leaves the completed production process as part of the finished consumption good. During its journey through the stages of production, no single physical object can be found in different stages at the same time. Therefore the actual outputs of any of these stages at a single moment in time are entirely independent of one another, they will ultimately

9

reach the consumer at different points in time as part of different units of the consumption good. This is illustrated in Fig. 1:

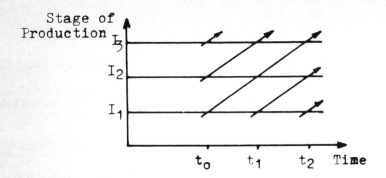

Fig. 1 : Time Structure of a Three–Stage Production Process
in a Lexis Diagram

In this Lexis diagram[1], time is measured on the horizontal axis, while the proximity to consumption (*"Konsumnähe"* in the terminology of Carl Menger (1871)) as denoted by the stages of production is measured along the vertical axis. The arrows running toward the upper right represent the path of a physical object through the stages of production. What prior to t_0 was a raw input to stage I_1 is transformed in that stage into a part of the intermediate product X_1 at t_0, from which it passes to I_2 for transformation into X_2 at t_1, and so on. It is clear that this sequential structure is preserved even if the object remains within a given stage of production for an infinitesimally small period of time. Just as no single object may be observed simultaneously at two different points in space, no input to the production of our consumption good may be observed simultaneously in two different stages of production; multi–stage production is a succession of processes, and not a unitary act compressed into a single moment in time[2].

---

[1]Lexis (1875) used a similar diagram to illustrate the age structure of a population. In Lexis' own diagram, the arrows which in Figure 1 go to the right are vertical, while the vertical lines of Figure 1 run diagonally from the upper left to the lower right in the original. It has, however, become common in applied demography to characterize constructions like that of Figure 1 as Lexis diagrams.

[2]In the context of Figure 1, simultaneous production would be represented by vertical arrows. Still, even at arbitrarily high velocities of production, the use of a sufficiently fine time scale would enable the succession of production steps to be correctly depicted as a sequential process.

In addition to following a given input on its way through the production process, Figure 1 may be used to provide two other perspectives. By cross–sectioning, the structure of production at any particular point in time can be depicted. Cutting through Figure 1 along the time axis, on the other hand, we observe the time path of output of any given stage of production. The quantitative relations between the cross–sections, the longitudinal cuts along the time axis and the diagonal cuts can be substantially illuminated by the principles of general system theory, and we shall later examine these relationships for the system of production equations to be sketched here and compare the results with those of existing economic theory. First, however, our example must be generalized step by step.

Embedded in our simple example are several restrictive assumptions. First, only one process takes place at each stage, so that the structure of production is entirely vertical, rather than horizontal. Second, all production steps are assumed to be of equal length. Third, all intermediates are held to flow unidirectionally toward consumption but not the other way round. Beyond this, it is assumed that none of the intermediate products is itself a consumption good, and finally, there is no joint production, so that there are no by–products to the production process[3]. As far as possible, we shall now relax these assumptions one at a time and observe the consequences.

Most simple is the introduction of several processes at any given stage of production. Consider a production path through stages H_1 and H_2 which exists parallel to the original path through I_1 and I_2 and whose products are combined with those of I_2 to produce the final consumption good in stage I_3. A three–stage production process of this kind is represented in Figure 2:

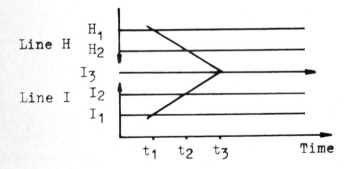

Fig. 2: Two Lines of Production on the First and Second Stages

For simplicity, only one production lot (viz., of those consumer goods

---

[3]These are, by and large, the assumptions underlying the older Austrian capital theory.

finished at time t_2) is depicted. In the first two stages, the independent industries I and H produce outputs which are combined in the third stage I_3. Deliveries between the industries I and H are easily represented by the dashed lines in Figure 2. However, a complete picture of the relations between the two industries requires a somewhat more complex Lexis diagram, incorporating a third dimension (Figure 3):

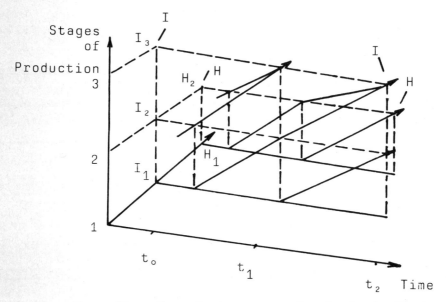

Fig. 3: Three–Stage Production with Two Production Lines

In Figure 3, the vertical axis once again describes the vertical structure of production, while the horizontal line to the rear separates the horizontal branches of production. Two production lots are represented where manufacturing starts at t_0 and t_1, respectively, and the process of production is equal to that of Figure 2. In this three–dimensional way, the notions of "horizontal" and "vertical" structures of production as economists ordinarily understand those terms can be portrayed.

Despite their heuristic value, these concepts quickly lose their power as we relax the remaining assumptions with which we began. Suppose we allow the time steps of production to vary in length, so that, for example, two time steps are required at stage I_2 to produce the intermediate commodity X_2. In the simplest case, labor and the intermediate good X_1 are required only during the first of these time steps, with the second used only for storage, perhaps for the ripening of the product. Then the flow of materials through the I–stages can be depicted as in Figure 4:

12

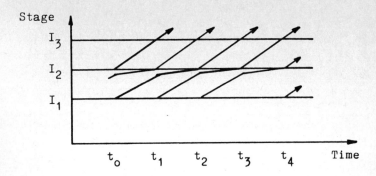

Fig. 4: Three–Stage Production with Doubled Production Period
in the Second Stage

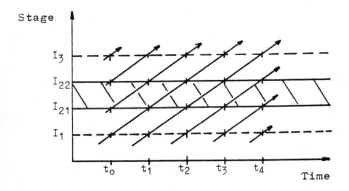

Fig. 5: "Three–Stage" Production With a Flow of Materials
Within the Second Stage

As can be seen, the products of two different lots are always in stage I_2 at the same time; thus, for example, at time t_3 the products fabricated at I_1 one time step before and the "ripened" products of the same stage at time t_1 are brought together in stage I_2. So there is in fact a flow of intermediates within stage I_2 which has been "lost" in the aggregation of Figure 4. It is, of course, possible to render this flow visible by disaggregating stage I_2 into substages I_{21} and I_{22} to produce Figure 5:

In Figure 5, the Lexis scheme regains its familiar shape, though the three–stage production schedule is replaced by one with four stages. But this points to a fundamental problem. The sequence of production stages may be defined according to either the number of exogenously chosen stages passed (which could be termed industry or stage–of–production approach) or the number of time steps passed (production period approach). The first way is followed by the input–output analysis of interindustry relations (after

13

Leontief (1941)), the second goes back at least to von Neumann (1937)[4]. In the analysis which follows, we shall identify the number of production steps (and along with that, the number of intermediate products) with the number of time steps. But when we move from discrete time to continuous time, we shall have to dispense with this convention, for as the number of time steps becomes infinite, the number of intermediates defined that way increases without bound along with it and the notion of intermediate products itself becomes meaningless[5]. This problem will be further discussed in Sec. 2.3. below.

There is yet another complication in Figure 4. As the intermediate product rests in stage I_2, it may be necessary to apply inputs a second time. Then, depending on the approach we have adopted to defining the sequence of production, we obtain either Figure 6a or Figure 6b:

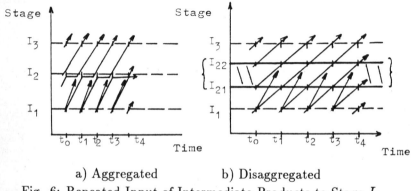

a) Aggregated   b) Disaggregated

Fig. 6: Repeated Input of Intermediate Products to Stage I_2

Consider Figure 6a first: As the products X_1 of time t_0 rest at stage I_2 they are processed a second time, at time t_2. For this purpose, repeated inputs of products X_1 are used, inputs which now belong to the production lot leaving from stage I_1 at time t_1. Thus, the produce of industry I_2 enters the production process of industry I_2 in two distinct ways. Because this double use of intermediate products would not reveal itself in empirical observation were the stage approach to be used, the production period approach must be employed to make it visible. Figure 6b makes explicit that at every moment, part of the product of stage I_1 is devoted to the further processing of goods

---

[4] A similar distinction is discussed by Hicks (1973). Burmeister (1974) shows that Hicks' approach is equivalent to von Neumann's; see also Beckmann (1971).

[5] I owe this point to Professor B. Schefold, University of Frankfurt.

stored in I_2 while the remainder is used for the current production of fresh goods in I_2.

In one sense, then, stage I_1 clearly lies before I_2, for the entire flow of materials flow from I_1 is directed to I_2. But at the very least, I_1 is not vertically prior to the substage I_{21}, for parts of the product of I_1 pass directly to stage I_{22}, without passing through I_{21}. To this extent I_1 is horizontal to I_{21}. The notion of horizontality in the production structure is similarly ambiguous. In the context of Figure 3, a branch of production H existed parallel to branch I such that both H_1 and I_1 and the stages H_2 and I_2 stood in a horizontal relationship to one another. If a doubled period of production is now introduced in stage I_2, however, this ordering is no longer unequivocal. In stage–of–production analysis, the sequence of production steps is left unchanged, while but from a production period point of view, stage H_2 can be seen as horizontal either to I_{21} or to I_{22}, depending upon whether we count stages from the beginning or from the end of the chain of production (Figures 7a and 7b):

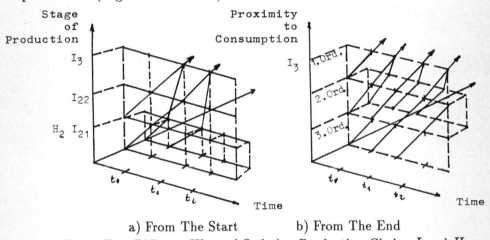

a) From The Start   b) From The End

Fig. 7 Two Different Ways of Ordering Production Chains I and H

In Figure 7a, we begin at the start of the production process, so that stages I_1 and H_1 are placed on the ground plane, that is, we regard them as horizontal. At the next stage along the path of production, we find I_{21} and H_2. Now before the products of lines I and H are combined to produce the consumption good in stage I_3, the products of industry I must pass another stage I_{22} while the output of H_2 enters directly into I_3. Therefore, two deliveries of raw materials which have been used as inputs to stages I_1 and H_1 at the same moment in time will reach the final stage of production, I_3, at different times. Just the reverse is observed in Figure 7b, in which the process is viewed from the other direction. Now the production of a particular lot of consumption goods is traced back through all the stages of production, so that the stages I_{22} and H_2 are horizontal to one another, as are the stages I_{21} and H_1. This is the perspective of Carl Menger (1871); in his terminology, the final consumption good is a "first order" good, the products of I_{22} and H_2 and those of I_{21} and H_1 are "second" and "third order" goods, respectively, with "fourth order" goods produced at stage I_1. Thus, while the various stages of production for any consumer good produced under such conditions must clearly begin at different points in time, the lack of a single, obviously superior means of ordering the production process leaves the labelling of the various stages as horizontal or vertical to one another purely a matter of taste.

A third assumption of our simple flow diagram was the well–defined flow of materials in a single direction through the stages of production, a postulate which has gained some celebrity in the discussion of Austrian capital theory. This restriction is lifted if we admit the possibility of material flows from stages "near" to the ultimate production of the comsumption good itself to stages which are more "distant" from this final process of manufacture, for instance, from stages I_2 tor I_3 back to I_1 (Figure 8):

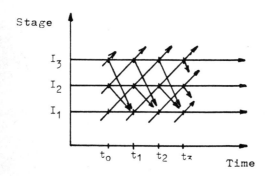

Fig. 8: Double Feedback in Three–Stage Production

This phenomenon is called "circularity" or "feedback"[6], and leads to three observations: First, each product which is recycled into earlier stages of production is directly or indirectly required for its own production, i.e. it can be said to reproduce itself. In Figure 8, for example, the products of stage I_1 are directed to stages I_2 and I_3 for further processing. But part of the outputs of stages I_1 and I_2 are themselves fed back into production at stage I_1. These recycled products of I_2 and I_3 thus take part in their own reproduction, the former indirectly over two stages, the latter directly in one.

---

[6] The older German–language discussion used the term *"Rückversetzung"*.

(An example of this is the use of energy produced in an electric power plant, which is then used in part itself to run the equipment in the plant which produced still more power.) The number of such intermediate steps in a given process of production may be large or small, and in the simplest case it falls to zero: The product then enters directly into its own production. In the theory of open systems, such circularity is sometimes called "autocatalysis", a term which is borrowed from chemistry[7].

Second, because the system as a whole is autocatalytic within the range of *Rückversetzung*, any stage of production may be taken as the point of departure for analysis, and after some number of iterations, every other stage of production will eventually be reached. Given the existence of feedback relationships, therefore, the notions of verticality and horizontality in production lose their meaning. Third, the presence of feedbacks makes it impossible to determine the period of production, the time any particular physical object remains within the sphere of production from resource extraction to final production of the consumption good. Since the flow of materials is no longer unidirectional, the attempt to calculate the period of production will result in an infinite regress; in principle, any given object may circulate endlessly within the range of *Rückversetzung* without ever leaving the sphere of production.

Even without feedback, the succession of production steps may become impossible to specify. Consider the case in which products are to be used both as consumption goods and as intermediate products. Here again the ordering of production stages as horizontal or vertical is arbitrary. Figure 9 illustrates such a case with three stages of production:

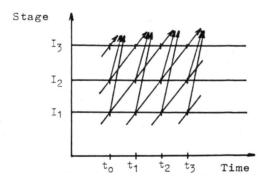

Fig. 9: Three–Stage Production With All Products As Consumption Goods

[7] von Neumann, whose pioneering 1937 study examined an entirely autocatalytic system, indeed held a degree in chemistry (received from *Eidgenoessische Technische Hochschule*, Zurich, in 1925).

In Figure 9, not only are the products of all stages themselves onsumption goods, but also the outputs of I_1 and I_2 are used as inputs to production further along the chain at I_2 and I_3, respectively. Seen through the lens of Menger's notion of proximity to consumption, all the stages of production are horizontal to one another, for each of them produces first–order goods. But at the sime time, they are vertical because they form a production chain where the outputs of I_1 and I_2 are used as inputs to production in the subsequent stage.

Finally we may consider the case of joint production. This is, we relax the assumption that in each stage, the process of production results in only one single output. In fact, there may be significant by–products at any stage of production, either in the form of waste or as outputs of tradable commodities. Suppose, for example, that the distinct outputs X_1 and X_3 are produced in stage I_1, while stages I_2 and I_3 produce the joint outputs (X_1, X_2) and (X_2, X_3), respectively. In this way, two stages always participate simultaneously in the production of each of three distinct products.

Within the confines of a simple Lexis diagram, it is impossible to portray both the interrelations of production stages and the interrelations of material flows at one and the same time. One possible solution to this problem is to disaggregate the production process by illustrating the sources of supply for each product separately, as in Figure 10:

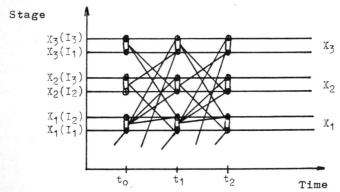

Fig. 10: Joint Production of Three Commodities in Three Stages

In Figure 10, we assume in addition that raw materials R_1 and intermediate outputs X_2 enter into stage I_1 while products X_1 and X_3 are used in stage I_2, and further that X_1 is an input to stage I_3. Now, because two separate stages must always contribute to the output of a commodity, the supply of every product must at all times be divided between six partial, elementary processes. We could, alternatively, have constructed Figure 10 so as to aggregate production processes instead of commodities, but this makes it impossible to depict graphically how supply of goods is divided among their uses in production at all times. Despite this difficulty, formal systems of commodity production choose this second method (see Sec. 2.1.3. and 2.2.3. below).

A special case of both *Rückversetzung* and joint production is presented by durable capital goods. Means of production of this kind are not physically represented in the output itself; rather, they act as catalysts and wear out after some period time. Like the intermediates of our first example they are produced commodities themselves and do not serve as consumption goods, this is, they never leave the sphere of production. Unlike these earlier products, only a part of their stock is lost in production while the remainder may be regarded as joint product (cf. von Neumann (1937), Sraffa (1960)). If, for example, stage I_1 requires the input of a durable capital good in quantity K_1, we may write:

$$I_1 : R_1 \oplus L_1 \oplus K_1 \qquad \longrightarrow \qquad X_1 \oplus (1 - \delta_1)K_1 \oplus Z_1$$

Here, $(1 - \delta_1)K_1$ is the quantity of the capital good left after the production step and Z_1 is the quantity of capital goods worn out that must be scrapped. Thus, $Z_1 = \delta_1 K_1$ where δ_1 is the loss rate of capital good 1.

In the Lexis diagram, the durability of capital goods may be represented as direct autocatalysis of the joint product K_1, as in Figure 11:

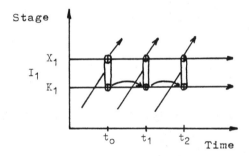

Fig. 11: Production by Means of Durable Equipment

In this Figure, K_1 is regarded as an intermediate product which is produced jointly with X_1 at stage I_1 and is reinserted into that same stage one time step later. The arrow going back to line K_1 represents this feedback of used machinery into the production process. In this context the loss rate per time step remains unknown. Technically it depends on the age of the equipment, on the intensity with which it is used, and on the kind of use to which it is put; two otherwise identical automobiles will wear out quite differently if one is used as a taxi while the other is driven only as a private car.

Let us now suppose that there are no fluctuations in employment or in the use of production capacity and that the distribution of equipment over all productions is constant[8]. Then the loss rate of a given production lot of capital goods is a function of their age. This relationship may be illustrated, as in Figure 12, in a life table, analogous to the life tables used in demography:

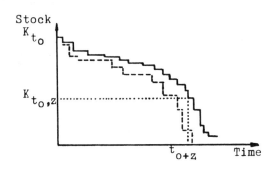

Fig. 12: Life Table For a Given Production Lot
of a Capital Good

Figure 12 shows the portion of a single cohort of capital goods which remain in useable condition after any given age. If the initial production at time t_0 is $K_{0,0}$, then $K_{0,z}$ units remain in useable condition at time $t_0 + z$.

In addition to this rate of technical loss, there exists a rate of economic loss, for it may be unprofitable to continue using old equipment, either because it consumes more raw materials and fuel than newer machines or because costs of maintenance and repair have come to exceed the value of the equipment itself. To determine rates of economic loss, prices and interest rates must be known, a possible scheme of economic survival is represented by the dashed lines in Figure 12. Machinery is most often scrapped before the moment of total technical loss. Hence the line of economic loss rates always lies below the line of technical loss rates, so that the latter is the envelope of the former. As long as the loss rate is not constant for all ages (which is the case with exponential depreciation), the age structure of equipment exerts an influence on the loss rate per time step: at a given moment in time, equipment of several different ages is in use, so that, for instance, a carrier whose fleet consists primarily of old trucks will face a technical loss

---

[8] For this restriction there is no justification other than mathematical convenience. Without it, we enter the slippery terrain of cause–specific life tables.

rate which differs from that of a carrier who owns mostly new vehicles. The age structure of a particular capital stock may once again be illustrated in a Lexis diagram (Figure 13):

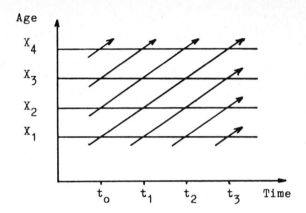

Fig. 13: Age Structure of Capital Stock in a Lexis Scheme

Figure 13 conforms to the simple scheme of Figure 1 above, but here, goods X_1 through X_4 are interpreted not as different commodities but as successive age classifications of a single good, though of course either interpretation makes sense. By cutting diagonally through Figure 13, separate life tables are obtained for each age cohort (Figure 14a). Because these age cohorts t_1, t_2 may differ in size, the loss rates per period of time obtained by cross section will generally differ from cohort loss rates, as shown in Figure 14b:

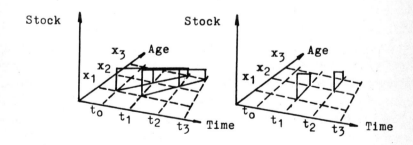

a) Vintage Life Table   b) Period Life Table
Fig. 14: Life Tables and the Lexis Diagram

21

In Figure 14 the ground plane is given by the axes of Figure 13. The vertical line measures the stocks of capital goods while the bars at intersections $(t_0; X_1), (t_1; X_2)$, and $(t_2; X_3)$ denote the stock of equipment of vintage t_0 left at each time between t_0 to t_2. The connecting lines between these columns in Figure 14a are nothing but the life tables of the lot of capital goods produced at t_0. The same is true for cohort t_1, illustrated from t_1 to t_3. Figure 14b repeats this illustration, but here the vertical bars are connected for a given point in time. These cross sections are a biased image of the cohort life tables in Figure 14a, representing loss rates per time step[9]. As Figure 14 shows, this bias is caused by the difference in size of cohorts K_{t_0} and K_{t_1}. Only in the stationary state the cross section through Figure 14 is an unbiased image of the technical loss rates.

This result may be generalized. We remember that in our example, the age classes x_1 to x_3 may be interpreted as different goods. Then, for each good the vertical axis of Figure 14 denotes the quantities produced. This leads us to the conclusion that the quantitative relationships between cross sections and cohort data which we found to exist for capital goods must hold also for commodities of any kind. In the next chapter it shall be shown algebraically that this is indeed the case. Before, however, we turn to the problem of price determination.

1.2. Price Equations

Prices result from one another in much the same way that products do; the prices of outputs depend, in some proportion, on the prices of the inputs used in production. Like production, moreover, price formation is a process which takes place over time. Those inputs which were used in yesterday's production had to be purchased at yesterday's prices, whatever the same commodities might cost today. Therefore, the supply price of output whose production was begun yesterday but not completed until today is determined by yesterday's input prices.

Because production proceeds in steps, producers face the problem of bridging the time span between the purchase of inputs and the sale of outputs; the production of goods to be sold tomorrow as finished products must be financed today, before the production process has begun. At several points in time, inputs of raw materials, intermediate products and of labor are required for which purchase on credit (which would only transfer the problem of finance to the previous stage of production) may not be possible. In a

---

[9] Figs. 14a and 14b are the analogues to cohort and period life tables in demography. Their formal representation can be traced back to Knapp (1868).

barter economy, such "prefinance" comprises all those finished goods which the producer must exchange today for inputs delivered: flour in exchange for the grain, shoes for the leather etc.; given to those suppliers who can or will not wait for payment until tomorrow, when the specific units of output resulting from their deliveries would be sold. The same may be true of the day laborer who must purchase his means of subsistence in order to work, although the peculiar nature of the labor contract may induce the employer to withhold the worker's wage as a security until the day's work is in fact completed. If all such relationships are traced back through the economy, an aggregate commodity is obtained which the classics called the subsistence fund[10]. In a monetary economy, the finance of production, like all economic transactions, is simplified. Now, prefinance consists of a sum of money which is either advanced to the producer on credit from the supplier or spent by the producer for inputs payable on delivery. So he who engages in multi-stage production must invest, the sum "vested in" commodities in this sense is called his circulating capital. Investment, therefore, begins here, it is not restricted to the act of installing machinery or other types of durable equipment[11].

Where there is investment, there is interest as well, charges for which the rational producer must always account in the price of his output. The sum necessary must either be advanced to the producer, in which case the lender will charge interest for its use, or the producer must meet his needs with his own funds, in which case investment will be made only if the producer expects it to yield at least the current rate of interest on these funds[12].

---

[10] The concept of a (fixed) subsistence fund was the cornerstone of most of the classical explanations of the division of income, the subsistence theories of wages.

[11] Perhaps the most extreme definition of capital in this sense is Böhm-Bawerk's (1889, Ch.2) who states that capital is the essence of all intermediate products ("*Kapital ist der Inbegriff aller Zwischenprodukte*").

[12] In the last century this consideration was common to the thinking of several diverse schools of thought. See, for example, Ricardo (1817), von Thünen (1826), J.St. Mill (1848), or later the labor theory of value of Marx (1859), as well as Jevons (1871) and the Austrians Menger(1871) and Böhm von Bawerk (1884, 1889). Formal treatments go back at least as far as von Bortkiewicz (1906, 1907) and Tugan–Baranovsky (1914). The modern discussion of price formation with circulating capital is grounded in von Neumann (1937) and Sraffa (1960). Reflecting the influence of Walras (1874) and J.B. Clark (1888), the element of time in price formation was no longer reckognized after the turn of the century, at least outside the Austrian school.

This leads to an important conclusion: The supply price of any commodity consists not just of the proportionate input prices, but of the interest charges which intervene between these goods as well. Interest is the premium without which no money would ever be made available for these timestaking processes of production. In commodity terms, this means that portions of the product are retained by the entrepreneur, the logical starting point for the theory of exploitation developed by Proudhon (1846), Marx (1849) and Rodbertus (1851).

Returning to the previous section's example of a three–stage production with commodities X_1, X_2, and X_3, we obtain Figure 15:

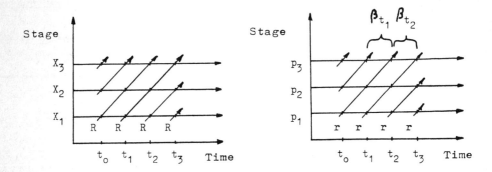

Fig. 15: Production and Price Formation
in Three Successive Production Steps

The diagram on the left in Figure 15 reproduces Figure 1. A consumer good X_3 is made from preliminary product X_2 which is in turn produced from X_1, all without feedbacks. All production steps are of equal length, so there is just one intermediate product per time step. Raw materials and/or labor are used at each stage of production, a point which is only indicated in Figure 15. Price formation follows the same principle, but interest charges are levied at each stage of production. On the vertical axis of the right–hand diagram of Figure 15, prices rather than quantities are represented. That which leaves the first stage at time t_1 had to have been produced beforehand with some expenditure of resources, so resource cost r_{1,t_0} must be included in price p_{1,t_1}. Without interest charges, the problem of price determination would now be solved: the equilibrium price of the commodity would equal the sum of its proportionate input prices. But the intervention of interest between input and output prices requires the definition of an interest factor $\beta_{1,t}$. If $b_{1,t-1}$ units of raw material are used to produce each unit of commodity 1, the price

---

On this point, see Hicks (1973).

24

of that commodity is:

$$p_{1,t} = \beta_{1,t}b_{1,t-1}r_{1,t-1}$$

Intermediate products $X_{1,t}$ undergo further processing at the second stage, that is, they enter production in quantity c_2 per unit of output. Together with resource prices r_2, resource input coefficients b_2 and the interest factor β_2, they determine the output price of commodity 2 as:

$$p_{2,t+1} = \beta_{2,t+1}(c_{2,t}p_{1,t} + b_{2,t}r_{2,t})$$

The same is true for production at the third stage one time step later.

The next production vintage, however, may be subject to very different price conditions, caused by fluctuations in demand relative to supply and manifested in resource prices $r_{1,t}$, $r_{2,t+1}$, $r_{3,t+2}$, and interest factors $\beta_{1,t+1}$, $\beta_{2,t+2}$, and $\beta_{3,t+3}$. Together these determine prices $p_{1,t+1}$, $p_{2,t+2}$, and $p_{3,t+3}$. None of these prices need correspond to the respective magnitudes which prevailed one period earlier. Depending on the direction of the price change, producers face capital gains or losses in their stocks of unfinished goods.

This example is easily extended to the case of circular productions. If there is feedback within production, product prices can no longer all be reduced to those of more basic products and resources. If, say, product X_1 indirectly produces X_3, X_3 produces X_1, they are inputs to one another corresponding to their input–output coefficients $c_{32} \cdot c_{21}$ and c_{13}. Therefore, their prices are also related in a circular way, as in Figure 16:

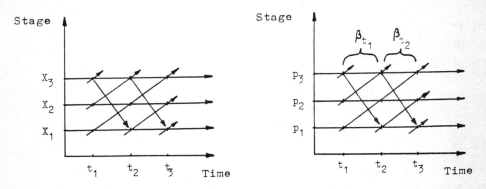

Fig. 16: Circular Production and Circular Price Formation

Note the differing lengths of the production chains from X_1 to X_3 and back from X_3 to X_1. This means that prices p_1 and p_3 do not enter into one another in relation to their input coefficients $\frac{c_{32} \cdot c_{31}}{c_{13}}$. Instead, an element of bias in their relationship is introduced by the interest factor β_{t1}. This is the basis of the so–called "transformation problem" to which we shall return in Sec. 3.3. below. The indirect commodity inputs in circular production lines form a decreasing geometric series, as do prices, so that circularities may be removed from price determination.

Nothing has been said thus far about how the prices of durable capital goods are formed. These may be understood as by–products in the production of intermediate products and consumer goods, as, in Figure 11 above, which is reproduced here as part of Figure 17:

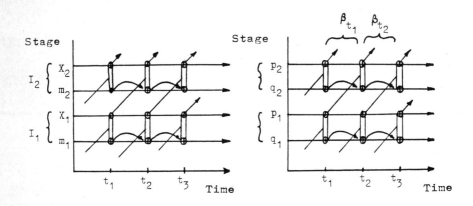

Fig. 17: Price Formation with Durable Equipment

The left–hand side of Figure 17 is simply Figure 11. Two industries manufacture four products: two finished goods, X_1 and X_2, and two kinds of machines $k_{1,z}$ and $k_{2,z}$ each of age z. Consider process I_1. Raw materials enter with prices $r_{1,t}$, and machines of age z and sales prices $q_{1,t,z}$ are used. At time $t+1$, products $X_{1,t+1}$, with prices $p_{1,t+1}$, appear along with machines of age $z+1$ with prices $q_{1,t+1,z+1}$. Note that the existence of industries I_3 and I_4, where these machines are themselves produced, must be assumed.

We might alternatively consider the prices of capital goods separately. At every point of time, some number of commodities is produced with the aid of the capital good. The price of the capital good is obtained by the sum of its future depreciation incomes. Given the prices of nondurable products, these user costs are in turn determined by the age–dependent input coefficients of the capital good in production. The stock of machines diminishes with increasing age, and as the analogue of this, their prices decline as well:

26

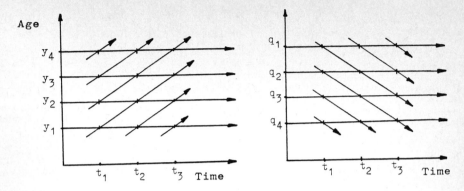

Fig. 18: Aging and Price Deterioration of Capital Goods

At time t, a new machine has price $q_{1,t,1}$, one time step later, it has the price of a "1–step–old" machine, $q_{1,t+1,2}$, and so on. There are both advantages and disadvantages to using older equipment. On the one hand, such equipment has already passed a part of its lifetime, and thus of its profitable employment, and this renders it cheaper. But on the other hand, it has already survived the risks inherent in its "childhood", and this tends to make it more expensive. Between them, these two effects effects (together with productive efficiency and maintenance cost, each of which depends upon age) determine the price of used equipment.

All this will be considered in detail in chapter 2. In Section 2.1.1., the time structure of quantities will be formalized, a task for which the basic equations underlying general system theory will be used. We shall see that these are equivalent to the results of a certain approach to dynamic input–output theory. Capital goods are taken into consideration in Section 2.1.2., where some tools of mathematical demography (itself a field of system theory) are used. Sec. 2.1.3. extends the analysis to the case of joint production. In Sec. 2.2., the price system, derived as a dual to the system of quantities, is examined. Section 2.2.2. once again takes respect of durable capital, and the problems of joint production are considered once more in Section 2.2.3.

2. The System of Economic Quantity and Price Equations

2.1. Quantity Equations

2.1.1. Production without Durable Equipment

2.1.1.1. Production Equations

We proceed now to formalize the ideas presented in the first chapter. As before, time is understood as a sequence of equidistant, discrete points $t_i, i \in Z$. Through these points in time, all events in the world are mapped into time space T, and we call the distance between two successive points in time a "time step"[1]. For the time being, we shall assume that no event occurs in less than one time step, so that no bias is introduced by the discrete representation of time. We shall relax this assumption later. We regard production as a transformation of resources into finished consumer through the application of human labor, and, in most cases, of previosly produced intermediate goods as well. Let $r = r_1, \ldots, r_m$ be an m–dimensional vector of raw–material inputs, some of which may denote the direct input of labor, and $c = c_1, \ldots, c_n$ be the n-dimensional vector of finished consumer goods. Both vectors are real and nonnegative. The transformation of inputs r into outputs of consumption goods c is achieved by a system of production Σ, the state of which is described by a n–dimensional state vector x. This vector spans a space $\Xi \subset R_0^{n+}$ which is called the "state space" (see e.g. Kalman/ Falb/Arbib (1968)), and the inflows r and outflows c similarly span the spaces $\Omega \subset R_0^{m+}$ and $\Gamma \subset R_0^{n+}$.

There are functional relations between the state variables, the inflows and the outflows. One may either regard the system state at time t as a recursion to the events at time t_1 or, alternatively, define the state of the variables r, x, and c at time t by their effect on x_{t+1}, the state of the system in the the subsequent point of time $t + 1$. The first alternative is called the "state-space" form of the system, while the second, which is more prevalent in economic theory, is called the "backward–recursive" form, see Luenberger/Arbel (1979). Scientific language in economics commonly refers to

---

[1]This sequence may be analogized to a stroboscope flashing at a given frequency. Note that the concept of discrete time employed here is different from the period analysis which is more common in economics. Here, t will be called a point in time, and $t_i - t_{i-1}$ a time step, although t is ordinarily regarded as a period of time. Both concepts, of course, are equivalent, but the period approach is occasionally prone to logical difficulties. A discussion of the period concept of time in economics is found in Baumol (1947), see also Samuelson (1947) and Frisch (1935).

this latter concept as "input–output theory", introduced by Leontief (1941). These relationships may be illustrated as in Figure 19:

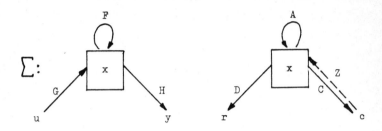

a) State–Space Representation   b) Input–Output Representation
Fig. 19: Two Forms of System Representation

Consider the state–space form first: There is a mapping, $G : u \mapsto x$, from the inputs, usually called u, to the state variables x, a second mapping of the state space into itself, $F : x \mapsto x$, and a mapping of the state variables into the outputs, $H : x \mapsto y$. The mapping rules F, G and H may be interpreted as semipositive matrices, so the state–space form of the system in discrete time becomes:

$$(2.1.1.) \qquad \Sigma : \quad \begin{aligned} x_{t+1} &= F_t x_t + G_t u_t \\ y_t &= H_t x_t \end{aligned}$$

As indicated by the time indices, the coefficients of matrices F, G and H may vary over time.

A clearer economic meaning can be attached to the system if its various terms are interpreted so that resource inputs r_t are understood to be the system's inflows u_t and finished consumer goods c_t to be its outflows y_t. Vector x_t thus becomes a vector of flows of intermediate commodities, and the system Σ as a whole describes the equations of motion of a commodity-producing economy[2]. The system (2.1.1.) must fulfill some conditions of consistency; one one of these which is important for our own discussions is

---

[2]Note that the notion of "output" in system theory differs from that in economics. In system theory, outputs are understood as the system outflows y, while in economic language, outputs ordinarily refer to everything which is produced within the system of production, that is, to the state vector x.

29

the decomposability of state transformations. A more general expression for the first equation in (2.1.1.) is:

(2.1.2.) $$x_{t+1} = \varphi(t; x_t, u_t)$$

and decomposability requires, see Kalman/Falb/Arbib (1968), that the state of the system at the subsequent point in time $t+2$, be dependent on its state at time t, so that:

(2.1.3.) $$x_{t+2} = \varphi_1(t+1; x_t, u_t)$$

is equivalent to two applications of the one–step state transformations:

(2.1.4.) $$x_{t+2} = \varphi(t+1; \varphi(t; x_t, u_t), u_{t+1})$$

This property guarantees the decomposability of longer production processes into a sequence of elementary steps, so that it makes no difference whether output at time $t+2$ is regarded as the outcome of a longer production process φ_1 beginning at time t or as the result of two successive one–step processes $\varphi \circ \varphi$ (Figure 20a). In Ch. 1 above the same decomposition was made in the context of a Lexis diagram (Figure 20b). It thus becomes possible to represent production processes of any kind and duration as a sequence of elementary processes, of which all have the same length:

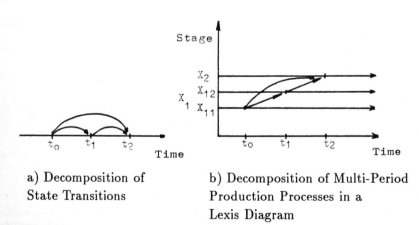

a) Decomposition of State Transitions

b) Decomposition of Multi-Period Production Processes in a Lexis Diagram

Fig. 20: Decomposability of State Transitions

Now consider the input–output form of system Σ, as illustrated in Figure 19b. It may at first seem unreasonable to add another form of system representation to the state–space form, but as we shall soon see, this makes sense when price systems are considered, for these are dual to the production system, more precisely, a backward–recursive (input–output) system of quantity equations has as its dual a forward–recursive system of price equations. Economic input–output analysis (backward–) recursively defines the state of a production system in terms of its effect on the system state one time step later, that is, mappings such as $D : x \mapsto r$ and $A : x \mapsto x$ are defined. The backward–recursive system is ordinarily completed by forward–recursive mappings from the output space to the state space $C : c \mapsto x$.

Once again, the mapping rules A, D, C may be regarded as semipositive matrices, so the economic interpretation of the backward–recursive system becomes:

(2.1.5a.) $$x_t = Ax_{t+1} + Cx_t$$

that is, the amount of intermediate commodities available at time t is divided between consumption at time t and further productive use until time $t + 1$. If the demand for consumer goods is treated as exogenous, then:

(2.1.5b.) $$x_t = Ax_{t+1} + c_t$$

Similarly, the inflow of raw materials and labor is divided into its various productive uses, so the input–output form of Σ is[3]:

(2.1.6.) $$r_t = Dx_{t+1}$$

It is interesting to ask under what conditions the input–output system (2.1.5–6.) collapses into the state–space form of Σ. Because there are more or fewer raw materials than fabricated products, matrix D is in general not square, and thus it is not invertible. A matrix $\mathcal{D} := \mathcal{G}$ must be defined such that:

(2.1.7.) $$x_{t+1} = Fx_t + \mathcal{D}r_t$$

In contrast, matrix A of (2.1.5.) is always square. In order to transform the backward–recursive system (2.1.5a.) into an ordinary (forward) difference

---

[3] The backward–recursive difference equation (2.1.5.) appears frequently in the literature. See Goodwin (1947), Chipman (1950), Metzler (1950). Exponential growth in such models has been examined by Solow (1952), Solow/Samuelson (1953) and, importantly, in the work of Nikaidô (1962, 1968). There, as well as in Orosel (1977), systems like (2.1.5b.) are considered as well.

equation, A must have the additional property of invertibility. Then (2.1.5a.) may be solved for x_{t+1}:

(2.1.8.) $$x_{t+1} = A^{-1}(x_t - Cx_t) = A^{-1}(I - C)x_t$$

and the input–output system becomes equivalent to the state–space form of Σ:
(2.1.9.)

$$\begin{aligned} x_{t+1} &= A^{-1}(I - C)x_t + Dr_t \\ c_t &= Cx_t \end{aligned} \qquad \text{where:} \qquad \begin{aligned} x &:= x \\ r &:= u \\ c &:= y \end{aligned} \qquad \begin{aligned} A^{-1}(I - C) &:= F \\ D &:= G \\ C &:= H \end{aligned}$$

That A must be invertible if the backward–recursive system (2.1.5a.) is to be solved for x_{t+1} was first demonstrated by Nikaidô (1962). The economic interpretation of this condition is, first, that for each comodity to be produced, inputs of intermediate goods are required (no column of A is zero), second, that each good serves as a production input, so that there are no pure consumption goods (no row of A is zero). Were it the case that one or more columns of A were zero, some goods would be manufactured directly from raw materials with the assistance of labor, a situation which, as the example of one– step production of services makes clear, might well arise in practice. The possibility of a row equal to zero, moreover, has attracted the attention of economists from Marx (1885) to Sraffa (1960). If there are pure consumption goods, then vector x may be so arranged that these goods are represented by its last $n - h$ elements. We denote these as $\tilde{x}$ and write:

(2.1.10.)
$$x_t = \begin{pmatrix} x_1 \\ \vdots \\ x_h \\ \tilde{x}_1 \\ \vdots \\ \tilde{x}_{n-h} \end{pmatrix}_t$$

Then the lower $n - h$ lines of matrix A remain empty, that is, pure consumption goods are not put into production:

(2.1.11.)
$$\begin{pmatrix} x_1 \\ \vdots \\ x_h \\ \tilde{x}_1 \\ \vdots \\ \tilde{x}_{n-h} \end{pmatrix}_t = \begin{bmatrix} A_1 & A_2 \\ \cdots & \cdots \\ 0 & 0 \end{bmatrix} \begin{pmatrix} x_1 \\ \vdots \\ x_h \\ \tilde{x}_1 \\ \vdots \\ \tilde{x}_{n-h} \end{pmatrix}_{t+1} + c_t$$

In Sraffa's terminology, the first h goods are "basic" commodities which, like pure consumption goods, may also be consumable. In addition to $c = Cx$ we define a (backward–recursive) mapping $Z : c \mapsto x$, in which Z is a diagonal matrix with the last $n - h$ diagonal elements as equal to unity:

$$(2.1.12.) \qquad Z = \begin{bmatrix} z_1 & & & & & 0 \\ & \ddots & & & & \\ & & z_h & & & \\ & & & 1 & & \\ & & & & \ddots & \\ 0 & & & & & 1 \end{bmatrix}_{n \times n} \qquad 0 \le z_i < 1$$

If Z is cut horizontally after row h, the resulting submatrices may be denoted as:

$$(2.1.13.)$$

$$Z_1 = \begin{bmatrix} z_1 & & 0 & \vdots & & \\ & \ddots & & \vdots & 0 & \\ 0 & & z_h & \vdots & & \end{bmatrix}$$

$$Z_2 = \begin{bmatrix} & & & \vdots & 1 & & 0 \\ & 0 & & \vdots & & \ddots & \\ & & & \vdots & 0 & & 1 \end{bmatrix}$$

so that the system (2.1.11.) may also be written as:
$$(2.1.14.)$$

$$\begin{pmatrix} x_1 \\ \vdots \\ x_h \\ \tilde{x}_1 \\ \vdots \\ \tilde{x}_{n-h} \end{pmatrix}_t = \begin{bmatrix} A_1 & A_2 \\ \cdots & \cdots \\ 0 & 0 \end{bmatrix} \begin{pmatrix} x_1 \\ \vdots \\ x_h \\ \tilde{x}_1 \\ \vdots \\ \tilde{x}_{n-h} \end{pmatrix}_{t+1} + \begin{bmatrix} Z_1 \\ \cdots \\ Z_2 \end{bmatrix} c_t$$

Finally, let the vector x be decomposed such that $x^{(B)}$ comprises all h basic commodities and $\tilde{x}$ the $n - h$ pure consumption goods. Then (2.1.14.) may be divided into two separate equation systems:

$$(2.1.15a.) \qquad x_t^{(B)} = A_1 x_{t+1}^{(B)} + Z_1 c_t + A_2 \tilde{x}_{t+1}$$
$$(2.1.15b.) \qquad \tilde{x}_t = Z_2 c_t$$

33

Insert b) into a) to find:

(2.1.16.)
$$x_t = A_1 x_{t+1} + Z_1 c_t + A_2 Z_2 c_{t+1}$$

A_1 is certainly invertible, so this problem at least is solved. But (2.1.16.) now becomes an implicit difference equation in both x and c which is insoluble for x_{t+1} (see Orosel (1977)). This difficulty in general arises because a subsystem is introduced when pure consumption goods are taken into consideration. Let Σ_B be the "basic system" of all goods which are essential inputs to production and Σ_{NB} be the "nonbasic" system of all pure consumption goods. Then the following relationships hold (Figure 21):

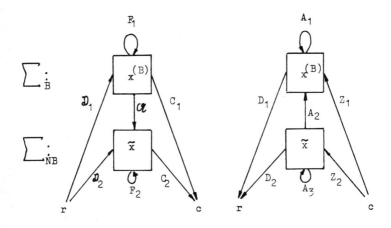

Fig. 21: Production with a Subsystem of Non–Basic Commodities

Written in the form of equations, the system in input–output form is:
(2.1.17.)
$$\begin{aligned}
\Sigma_B : \quad & x_t^{(B)} = A_1 x_{t+1}^{(B)} + Z_1 c_t + A_2 \tilde{x}_{t+1} \\
\Sigma_{NB} : \quad & \tilde{x}_t = Z_2 c_t \quad (+ \quad A_2 \tilde{x}_{t+1}) \\
& r_t = D_1 x_{t+1}^{(B)} + D_2 \tilde{x}_{t+1}
\end{aligned}$$

while the state–space form is given as:
(2.1.18.)
$$\begin{aligned}
\Sigma_B \quad & x_{t+1}^{(B)} = A_1^{-1}(I - C_1)x_t - A_2 \tilde{x}_{t+1} + D_1 r_t \\
& c_t = C_1 x_t^{(B)} + C_2 \tilde{x}_t \\
\Sigma_{NB} : \quad & \tilde{x}_{t+1} = A x_t + D_2 r_t \quad (+ \quad F_2 \tilde{x}_t) \\
& c_t = C_2 \tilde{x}_t + C_1 x_t^{(B)}
\end{aligned}$$

Because in general there are different numbers of basic commodities and of consumption goods, an inverse for A_2 does not exist, and so a matrix $\mathcal{A}$ must be defined instead.

The system of non–basics can easily (see Orosel (1977)) be generalized by a local flow of intermediates $A_3 : \tilde{x} \mapsto \tilde{x}$. This does not alter the properties of subsystem Σ_{NB} even if A_3 is once again not invertible, for otherwise there would be no pure consumption goods.

The state–transition functions $x_{t+1} = Fx_t + Gu_t$ which underlie equations such as (2.1.18.) have their economic counterparts in the production functions. There, however, the additive form is unusual. Either fixed coefficients are used such that:

$$(2.1.19.) \qquad\qquad x_{t+1} = \min\left(Fx_t; Gu_t\right)$$

or variable coefficients are employed with the properties:

$$(2.1.20.) \qquad x_{t+1} = f(Fx_t; Gu_t) \quad \begin{array}{l} f'_x, f'_y > 0 \\ , f''_x, f''_y < 0 \\ \lambda^m f(x; u) = f(\lambda x; \lambda u) \end{array}$$

In this context the fact that production takes time is often neglected; only seldomly time indices are given for production functions, (an important exception is e.g. Burmeister/Sheshinski (1968) and Burmeister/Dobell (1970)).

2.1.1.2. Observation Equations

We have seen in Chapter 1 that biases may arise when multi–stage processes are cross–sectioned at a given moment in time, and we now turn to this problem. For a dynamic system, mappings other than the equations of motion may be defined. These mappings denote the relationships between the system quantities at a given time t. Viewed from the perspective of a Lexis diagram, such mappings are equivalent to cross–section observation. By analogy to (2.1.5.), we obtain:

$$(2.1.21.) \qquad \begin{array}{l} \hat{A}: \quad x_t \mapsto x_t \\ \hat{D}: \quad r_t \mapsto x_t \end{array}$$

The rules defining these mappings may be regarded as cross–section input–output matrices. The typical element $\hat{a}_{ij}$ of $\hat{A}$ denotes the input of intermediate product i per unit of the simultaneously produced good j. A similar analogy applies for raw–material inputs and the elements $\hat{d}_{kj}$ of cross–section

35

matrix $\hat{D}$. From these matrices, observation equations may be derived[4]. Let us begin by neglecting consumption. The observation equation for the flow of intermediate goods at time t is then:

(2.1.22.) $$x_t = \tilde{A}_t$$

i.e.

(2.1.23.) $$(I - \tilde{A})x_t = 0$$

where I is the identity matrix and 0 the n–dimensional null vector. (2.1.23.) is the form of the closed static model of Leontief (1941)[5]. The observation of the inflow of resources is:

(2.1.24.) $$r_t = \hat{D}x_t$$

or, from a productivity perspective:

(2.1.25.) $$x_t = \hat{D}r_t$$

We now introduce labor inputs l_t as distinct from resource inputs. The apparent labor productivity then is:

(2.1.26.) $$x_t = \tilde{\mathcal{E}}l_t \quad ,$$

a semipositive h–dimensional column vector. Taken together, (2.1.22-26.) form the Leontief production function:

(2.1.27.) $$x_t = \min\left(\hat{A}^{-1}x_t; \hat{D}r_t; \hat{\mathcal{E}}l_t\right)$$

If consumption is now taken into account, the observation equation is generalized to:

(2.1.28.) $$x_t = \hat{A}x_t + c_t$$

---

[4] This to some extent a misuse of system–theoretic terminology, for it is common to identify an observation equation with the external system description $y_t = Hx_t + Ju_t$. For the time being, we shall assume that every cross–section is an observation equation; the examination of system observability in the proper sense is postponed until Section 2.3. below.
[5] The dynamics of Leontief's models are considered in Section 3.1. below.

which is just the open Leontief model (Leontief (1951)):

$$(2.1.29.) \qquad x_t = (I - \hat{A})^{-1}c_t$$

Matrix $(I - \hat{A})^{-1}$ is commonly called the Leontief inverse. From this, the apparent production function in cross–section data becomes:

$$(2.1.30.) \qquad x_t = \min(\hat{A}^{-1}(I - C)x_t; \hat{D}r_t; \hat{E}l_t)$$

There are countless empirical estimations of such stationary Leontief models in which the underlying time series are not stationary, but biases unvariably arise in such cases; and we shall later see that under certain conditions these biases will be systematic. First, however, we shall try to deepen our understanding of the difference between cross–section and dynamic analysis of a system of production. Returning to the example of a Lexis diagram with three successive stages of production, we have Figure 22:

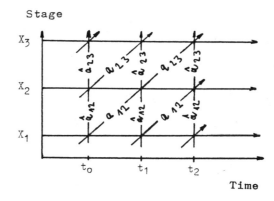

Fig. 22: Observation and Production Coefficients in a Lexis Diagram

We assume in Figure 22 that a consumption good is produced in three steps without feedbacks and with no account taken of the inflows of raw materials and labor. Following the flow of intermediates through all stages of production from time t_0 to time t_1, we obtain the technical coefficients $a_{12} = x_{1,t_0}/x_{2,t_1}$ and $a_{23} = x_{2,t_0}/x_{3,t_1}$, each of which is independent of the quantities produced[6]. In the particular case of constant coefficients, it makes

---

[6]We might alternatively assume nonzero returns to scale without affecting the conclusions.

37

no difference whether a particular production vintage is followed from, say, t_0 to t_2 or two vintages are observed from t_0 to t_1 instead. If, for example, a_{12} measures the input of rubber per tire in automobile production and a_{23} represents the number of tires per car, these relations remain constant, irrespective of whether two successive steps or two parallel steps of production are considered. But this invariance does not apply to the observation coefficients $\hat{a}_{ij}$, which are the ratio of today's rubber output to today's tire production, $\hat{a}_{12} = x_{1,t}/x_{2,t}$, and the ratio of tires produced today to automobiles produced today, $\hat{a}_{23} = x_{2,t}/x_{3,t}$. If the factory is to produce 1,000 cars today and 1,100 cars tomorrow, 5,000 tires must have been supplied yesterday and another 5,500 today (our plant is still conservative enough to supply the traditional spare tire). Now if today's output of 5,500 tires is compared to today's output of 1,000 cars, we observe a ratio of 5.5 tires per car; were automobile production to be increased by 20%, the resultant ratio would be 6.0, and so on. A bias, then, is apparently introduced when the technical structure of production is estimated by cross–section data; the observed coefficient $\hat{a}_{ij}$ is the product of the technical coefficient and the proportionate expansion of production. We shall now generalize this observation for the case in which all productions grow at the same rate.

2.1.1.3. Balanced Growth I:
Accumulation of Intermediate Products

Balanced (exponential) growth means that all quantities in the economic system expand at the same rate. Let α be the von Neumann coefficient of expansion of the economy (von Neumann (1937)). Then the state vectors of two subsequent points in time are connected by:

(2.1.31.)
$$x_{t+1} = \alpha x_t$$

Insertion into (2.1.5a.) yields:

(2.1.32.)
$$(2.1.32.)x_t = \alpha A x_t + C x_t$$

and[7]:

(2.1.33.)
$$(I - C - \alpha A)x_t = 0$$

With balanced growth, the production coefficient a_{ij} becomes:

(2.1.34.)
$$a_{ij} = \frac{x_{ij,t}}{x_{j,t+1}} = \frac{x_{ij,t}}{\alpha x_{j,t}}$$

---

[7]On the existence of positive solutions for x_t, see Nikaidô (1968); a more general proof is Vahrenkamp (1977).

where x_{ij} is the quantity of product i introduced into the production of commodity j. Compare this to the observerd coefficient:

$$(2.1.35.) \qquad \hat{a}_{ij} = \frac{x_{ij,t}}{x_{j,t}}$$

to find:

$$(2.1.36.) \qquad \hat{a}_{ij} = \alpha a_{ij}$$

This makes clear that, as suggested above, the observed coefficient is the product of the technical coefficient and the proportionate expansion of production.

Balanced growth also means the expansion of resources and labor inputs, as well as consumption, by factor α:

$$(2.1.37.) \qquad \begin{aligned} l_{t+1} &= \alpha l_t \\ r_{t+1} &= \alpha r_t \\ c_{t+1} &= \alpha c_t \end{aligned}$$

(Note that this is the equivalent of cutting along the time axis in a Lexis diagram). The input–output coefficients of raw materials and labor, d_{kj} and e_{hj}, are thus biased as well when measured in cross–section analysis. So:

$$(2.1.38.) \qquad \begin{pmatrix} \hat{A} \\ \hat{D} \\ \hat{E} \end{pmatrix} = \alpha \begin{pmatrix} A \\ D \\ E \end{pmatrix}$$

The reverse is true for the observed values of the productivity matrices:

$$(2.1.39.) \qquad \begin{pmatrix} \hat{D} \\ \hat{\mathcal{E}} \end{pmatrix} = \frac{1}{\alpha} \begin{pmatrix} D \\ \mathcal{E} \end{pmatrix}$$

In sum, we note that with steady–state growth, every technical input–output matrix must be multiplied by α in order to find its cross–section estimator, while the productivity matrices collapse into their estimators when multiplied by the reciprocal $\frac{1}{\alpha}$. Since all these mappings which relate technical to observed coefficients have fixed points for the stationary state of the system, the true technical coefficients of production can be obtained from the observation of cross– sectional data by simply adjusting those data on the basis of von Neumann's factor of expansion.

39

Before moving to a consideration of the price system, we must consider the further generalizations of the quantity system suggested by the introduction of both capital goods and joint products. But because the appropriate way to treat the formalization of capital goods in particular is less than perfectly clear, we shall have to approach our central questions in a somewhat roundabout way.

2.1.2. Production with Durable Capital Goods

2.1.2.1. Production Equations

In the last section, we examined the time structure of production in the case of intermediate goods alone. Now, we extend the analysis to include durable capital goods. In principle, such commodities (which are ordinarily such material commodities as buildings and machinery but which might be intangible resources as well) appear in the flow of intermediates. Like these intermediate goods, they are products which are themselves used in the process of production. But unlike intermediate goods as we have defined them, durable capital goods are not incorporated by the production process into the finished product; instead, they survive several repetitions of the process to wear out after some period of time.

There are to ways to include such durables into system Σ. One is simply to regard them as intermediates, treating them as joint products such that each capital good is conceptually decomposed into as many different goods as there are age groups passed, a strategy employed already by David Ricardo[8].

A second approach, rooted in the productivity theories of capital and first elaborated formally by Léon Walras (1877), is to construct a subsystem Σ_K connected with the flow of intermediate goods. Walras' version, though valid only under most restrictive conditions, has long been predominant[9].

In both this section and the corresponding section on prices below, this second general strategy will be pursued; capital goods will be treated as a separate subsystem, but because we shall dispense with Walras' assumptions, our principal results will be different from his. The equivalence of our approach to the joint–production method will be shown in Section 3.2. below.

Let there be q different types of durable means of production p, $p = 1,\ldots,q$. The existing stock of each type at time t is denoted $k_{p,t}$ and is

---

[8] A similar way of reasoning was adopted by the Austrians, especially Böhm von Bawerk (1889). It was formalized by von Neumann (1937) and introduced in the context of a general theory of value by Sraffa (1960). For a modern treatment of this field, see Schefold (1979).

[9] A modern representation of Walras' system with durable capital goods is found in Morishima (1964).

measured in arbitrary quantity units or, more simply, in numbers of pieces. Each of these stocks $k_{p,t}$ is in itself an aggregate composed of capital goods of various vintages; it contains the sum of the production capacities of type p ready for operation at time t, each unit distinguished by its construction date $t - z$, where z is the age of a given piece of equipment. Taken together, these stocks k_p form a q–dimensional vector k which spans a space $K \in R^{q+}$, which is itself the state space of subsystem Σ_K.

This subsystem may be regarded as a population of stocks k_p with z age cohorts and q types. Some useful results of demography can be applied to this population. Let $y_{p,t-z}$ be the new production of capital goods of type p at time t. Not all the members of this cohort of equipment survive to age z, for some of will have failed or have been scrapped prior to this time. The fraction of vintage $t - z$ which survives to the age of z will be called $l_{p,z}$. For the moment, we shall assume that all equipment is used over the entirety of its technical lifetime[10]. although we shall examine below the conditions under which this assumption must be relaxed. The size of cohort p, t_z after z periods is thus:

$$(2.1.40.) \qquad\qquad k_{p,t,z} = y_{p,t-z} l_{p,z}$$

The stock of all capital goods existing of type p is obtained by summing (2.1.40.) over all age groups z, this is, over all cohorts or dates of construction $t - z$:

$$(2.1.41.) \qquad\qquad k_{p,t} = \sum_{z=1}^{w} y_{p,t-z} l_{p,z}$$

The minimum and maximum ages are 1 and w, respectively. Because at least one time step elapses between the construction of the good and its first use in production, each capital goods must be at least one period old, and we shall see that it facilitates the analysis to assume a maximum age w.

The sequence of survival rates l_z merits further consideration. If a fraction $m_{p,z}$ of the equipment fails between ages $z - 1$ and z, the stock of age z can be obtained from the stock of age $t - 1$:

$$(2.1.42.) \qquad k_{p,t,z} = (1 - m_{p,z}) k_{p,t-1,z-1} \qquad , \qquad m_{p,z} \geq 0$$

where $m_{p,1} = 0$ and $m_{p,w+1} = 1$. The first condition, $m_{p,1} = 0$, means that all freshly produced equipment is indeed put into operation, so that it

---

[10]This is the first of the restrictive assumptions at the base of Walrasian theory. See also Section 3.1. below.

41

is not neccesary to further distinguish between successful and unsuccessful production of capital goods. The second condition, $m_{p,w+1} = 1$, implies that all capital goods wear out at the maximum age w, though for some types of equipment the maximum lifetime is much shorter; that is, there are technically different ages $s < w$ such that for all $u > s$, $m_{p,u} = 0$. Now the survival rate $l_{p,z}$ is the cumulation of all one–period survival rates for the earlier ages $v < z$:

$$(2.1.43.) \qquad l_{p,z} = \prod_{v=1}^{z} (1 - m_{p,v}) = l_{p,z-1}(1 - m_{p,z})$$

From this it follows that the $l_{p,z}$ get smaller with increasing age:

$$(2.1.44.) \qquad l_{p,z} \geq l_{p,z+1} \qquad z = 1, \ldots, w+1$$

where the strict inequality must hold at least for $l_{p,w+1}$, in which case the so–called "rectangular life table" is obtained (otherwise the life table resembles descending stairs of unequal lengths).

Thus far, we know what fraction of a given vintage fails per time step, but we do not yet know how much of the total stock of commodity p, $k_{p,t}$, has been lost. This stock is the sum of all vintages of p currently in use, and so the overall loss rate must be a weighted average of the age–specific loss rates. We denote this unknown as δ_p, a variable which clearly depends on the age structure of stock $k_{p,t}$. The stock of good p at time t is equal to the inflow of newly installed equipment, minus losses, plus the surviving stock of the preceding period:

$$(2.1.45.) \qquad k_{p,t+1} = y_{p,t} + (1 - \delta_{p,t})k_{p,t}$$

After changing time indices, we use the definition for the stock of type p, (2.1.41.), to find:

$$
\begin{aligned}
(2.1.46.) \qquad k_{p,t+1} &= \sum_{z=1}^{w} y_{p,t+1-z} l_{p,z} \\
&= \sum_{z=1}^{w+1} y_{p,t+1-z} l_{p,z}
\end{aligned}
$$

since $l_{p,w+1} = 0$ because w is the maximum attainable age.

Moreover, because (2.1.43.) implies:

$$l_{p,z} = l_{p,z-1}(1 - m_{p,z}) \qquad ,$$

successive insertion into (2.1.46.) yields:

(2.1.47a.) $\quad k_{p,t+1} = \sum_{z=1}^{w+1} y_{p,t+1-z} \cdot l_{p,z-1}(1-m_{p,z})$

(2.1.47b.) $\qquad = y_{p,t}(1-m_{p,1}) + \underbrace{\sum_{z=2}^{w+1} y_{p,t+1,z}l_{p,z-1}}_{k_{p,t}}$

$$\underbrace{-\sum_{z=2}^{w+1} y_{p,t+1-z}l_{p,z-1} \cdot m_{p,z}}_{-\delta_{p,t}k_{p,t}}$$

The third term in (2.1.47b.) is the solution of $-\delta_{p,t}k_{p,t}$, the loss of equipment between t and $t+1$. This is easily seen once the indices are changed: (2.1.47c.)

$$k_{p,t+1} = y_{p,t}(1-m_{p,1}) + \sum_{v=1}^{w} y_{p,t-v}l_{p,v}$$

$$-\sum_{v=1}^{w} y_{p,t-v}l_{p,v} \cdot m_{p,v+1}$$

where $v := z-1$. Employing the assumption $m_{p,1} = 0$ and equation (2.1.42.) we obtain :

$$k_{p,t+1} = y_{p,t} + (1-\delta_{p,t})k_{p,t}$$

from (2.1.47c.), and the loss rate is found to be:

(2.1.48.) $\qquad \delta_{p,t} = \dfrac{1}{k_{p,t}} \sum_{z=1}^{w} y_{p,t-z}l_{p,z} \cdot m_{p,z+1}$

The stock of capital goods and the flows of intermediate goods interact in two ways. First, newly produced equipment is added to the stocks and, second, certain quantities of capital goods must be present in commodity production. The system of intermediate goods, which we shall call Σ_x, thus has two outflows, consumer goods c and investment goods y, the first of which leave the production sphere entirely while the latter enter into subsystem Σ_K. Within the system of intermediates, it is useful to distinguish between the manufacture of commodities in general and of capital goods in particular.

43

No further material flows exist between the two subsystems; the production of commodities requires the presence of durable capital goods. These act on the volume of output as a catalyst, and the extent of their capacity acts as a constraint on possible output.

But machines and other capital equipment do not physically enter into the ultimate product. For each production run, the services of a certain number of machines of a particular kind are required per unit of output, a value which may be expressed either in terms of productive capacity or its reciprocal, the elapsed time per unit of output. Taken together, these relationships yield Figure 23:

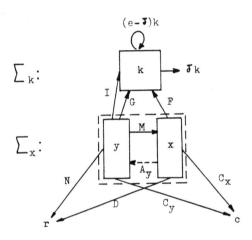

Fig. 23: Production System with Durable Capital Goods

Fig. 23 represents the interactions between the various components of the system, with most of them given in input–output form. Once again, we shall interpret the mappings so defined as matrices. Consider first the material flow within the system of capital goods Σ_K. If the period loss rates $\delta_{p,t}$ are known, the flow of goods within this sytem is completely determined. Together with the inflows y, the state–transition function of subsystem Σ_K is:

(2.1.49.) $$k_{t+1} = F_{(K)}k_t + G_{(K)}y_t$$

44

where $F_{(K)}$ and $G_{(K)}$ are given as[11]:

$$(2.1.50) \qquad F_{(K)} = (I - I\delta_t)k_t = (e - \delta_t) * k_t \quad , \delta_t = \begin{pmatrix} \delta_1 \\ \vdots \\ \delta_q \end{pmatrix}$$

$$(2.1.50b.) \qquad G_{(K)} = I$$

Here e is the q–dimensional unit vector[12].

Insofar as the material flow within the system of intermediates Σ_x is now segregated, we distinguish between the manufacture of semi–finished goods and the production of durable equipment:

$$(2.1.51.) \qquad x_t = Ax_{t+1} + My_{t+1} + Cx_t$$

The same distinction is applied to raw–material inputs:

$$(2.1.52.) \qquad r_t = Dx_{t+1} + Ny_{t+1}$$

If (2.1.45.) is put into its backward–recursive form, the use of investment goods is given as:

$$(2.1.53.) \qquad y_t = k_{t+1} - k_t + \delta_t * k_t$$

where it is implicitly assumed that investment goods may be used neither as intermediates nor as consumption goods. This assumption may be relaxed by defining matrices A_y and C_y such that:

$$(2.1.54.) \qquad y_t = A_y x_{t+1} + k_{t+1} - (e - \delta_t) * k_t + c_y y_t$$
$$\text{where}$$

$$A_y = [a_{pj}]_{q \times n} \quad , \quad C_y = \begin{bmatrix} \kappa_1 & & 0 \\ & \ddots & \\ 0 & & \kappa_q \end{bmatrix} < I$$

In general, A_y is not square (that is, not all investment goods are useful as intermediates, and vice versa); if A_y is quadratic and invertible then there is no difference between capital goods and intermediates.

---

[11]In the following we shall frequently refer to $a * b \equiv (a_i \cdot b_i)_{n \times 1}$ as the dot product of two vectors. We shall meet the convention that scalar multiplication is to be exerted before logical multiplication.

[12]δ or $(e - \delta)$ may also be regarded as diagonal matrices.

While these considerations determine the material flows within the productive system as a whole, it remains to see just how capital goods affect production. Between the stocks of equipment and the output of intermediates and investment goods there is an array of passage coefficients such that:

$$(2.1.55.) \qquad k_t = F x_{t+1} + G y_{t+1}$$

(Note that the input–output matrices F and G must not be confused with the matrices F and G defined by generalized state–transition functions). The coefficients of F and G have the dimension:

$$\frac{k_{pi}}{x_i} \text{ resp. } \frac{k_{ps}}{y_s} \; \hat{=} \; \frac{\text{number of pieces installed of equipment p}}{\text{output of commodity } i \text{ resp. of investment good } s/\Delta t} \; ,$$

that is, they denote the reciprocal of a production capacity per unit of time. If the number of pieces of equipment in the numerator is set equal to one, the result is the elapsed time of production for a single unit of output produced on equipment p.

A second way to represent the interrelations between stocks and flows is to figure loss rates δ_t into production such that:

$$(2.1.56.) \qquad \delta_t * k_t = H x_{t+1} + J y_{t+1}$$

Addition of k_t yields:

$$(2.1.57.) \qquad k_t = H x_{t+1} + J y_{t+1} + (e - \delta_t) * k_t$$

For the stocks of any production vintage $t - z$ the same calculation leads to:

$$(2.1.58.) \qquad k_{t,z} = H x_{t+1,z} + J y_{t+1,z} + k_{t+1,z+1}$$

where summation of the x_z and y_z over all vintages k_{t-z} yields total outputs x and z.

Thus far, we have implicitly assumed that all equipment of type p have the same productivity, irrespective of their age. We now relax this assumption. Let $k_{t,z}$ be the stock vector of equipment of age z and of all types p. Then for each of the z age cohorts there is a particular production technique with age–dependent coefficients:

$$(2.1.59) \qquad k_{t,z} = F_z x_{t+1,z} + G_z y_{t+1,z}$$

where x_z and y_z are the quantities produced in those processes which use equipment of age z. Nor are these coefficients the only ones which change. Machines and other equipment are the place where intermediate goods, raw materials and human labor are "combined" in production. As the technical characteristics of productive equipment vary, the input coefficients of all other means of production vary as well; an older machine performs more poorly than a newer one, and needs more energy and maintenance even without technical progress. There are thus z age–specific production techniques:

$$(2.1.60.) \qquad x_{t+1,z} = f_z(A^{-1}(I - C)x_t; \mathcal{F}_z k_{t,z}; \mathcal{D}_z r_{t,z}), \quad z = 1, \ldots, w$$

for intermediate goods and z age–dependent techniques for the production of capital goods:

$$(2.1.61.) \qquad y_{t+1,z} = g_z(\mathcal{M}_z x_{t,z}; G_z^{-1} k_{t,z}; \mathcal{N}_z r_{t,z}), \quad z = 1, \ldots, w$$

Both of these equations may be interpreted as state–transition functions for the age–dependent system $\Sigma_{x,z}$. Since the input–output matrices F, D, M and N are not invertible, suitable matrices $\mathcal{F}, \mathcal{D}, \mathcal{M}$ and $\mathcal{N}$ must be defined.

Of course, there is no reason why all equipment employed in the production of a single good must be of equal age; in a metal–working factory, for example, recently installed machine tools may be combined with electric power supplies and the like which were installed long ago, and this may exert an influence on their performance. So the average production technique of commodity i is not simply a linear combination of the z–techniques. In the aggregate, there may be productions s where s is an arbitrary age composition of the capital stock:

$$(2.1.62.) \qquad k_{t,s} = F_s x_{t+1,s} + G_s y_{t+1,s}, \ k_{t,s} = \begin{pmatrix} \sum_{r=1}^{w} k_{1,r} \\ \vdots \\ \sum_{u=1}^{w} k_{p,u} \\ \vdots \\ \sum_{v=1}^{w} k_{q,v} \end{pmatrix}_{t,s}$$

Here u, v, w are arbitrary age groups. It is clear that matrices F_s and G_s need not be linearly dependent on F_z and G_z. Along with these matrices, there exist input–output matrices A_s, M_s, N_s, D_s for all age compositions s, and these are also linearly independent of the z–techniques. Thus the aggregate production technique depends not only on the age structure of capital goods as a whole but on their distribution over all industries as well. We shall avoid this complication by assuming that only z–techniques are used, that is, equipment of different ages are not combined in production[13].

To this point, durable means of production have been treated as if they were completely isolated from the flows of intermediates; once a piece of equipment is installed, it requires no maintenance, no repair or replacement. We now dispense with this restriction and assume that inputs of service parts x and machines k are required to maintain a piece of equipment of age z. The generalized input equations in input–output form are thus:

$$(2.1.63.) \qquad x_t = Ax_{t+1} + \sum_{z=1}^{w} F_z^{(-)} k_{t+1,z} + My_{t+1} + c_t$$

$$(2.1.64.) \qquad k_t = Fx_{t+1} + \sum_{z=1}^{w} G_z^{(-)} k_{t+1,z} + Gy_{t+1}$$

In these equations, aggregate production techniques are given, so that the matrices depend on the age structure of the capital stock:

$$(2.1.65.) \qquad F = \sum_{z=1}^{w} \frac{k_{p,z}}{k_p} f_{pi,z} \quad , \quad G = \sum_{z=1}^{w} \frac{k_{p,z}}{k_p} g_{pq,z}$$

where $f_{pi,z}$ and $g_{pq,z}$ denote the number of p–machines of age z used per unit of good i and equipment q, respectively. the aggregation of coefficients $a_{ij,z}$, $f_{pi,z}^{(-)}$, $g_{pq,z}^{(-)}$ and $m_{pq,z}$ is more difficult. Here, the assumption of given z–techniques is required, that is, aggregate production must be decomposable into z–processes. Then, for example, the typical element a_{ij} of matrix A may be represented as:

$$(2.1.66.) \qquad a_{ij} = \sum_{z=1}^{w} \frac{x_{j,z}}{x_j} a_{ij,z}$$

Analogous results obtain for coefficients $f_{pj,z}^{(-)}$ and $m_{ip,z}$.

We come now to the case where technical loss rates are replaced by economic ones. By and large, durable equipment is scrapped before the end

----

[13] It should be noted that this is equivalent to a straightforward application of the joint–production approach. It does not seem to be possible to proceed without distinguishing processes from products. z–techniques, incidentally, must also be assumed when durables are considered joint products. See Section 3.2. below.

of its operative lifetime if its continuous use would mean waste of costly goods which could be reduced or eliminated by the installation of a new one. This might be due either to an age–dependent rise in the consumption of fuels and raw materials per unit produced or to costs of service and repair that exceed expected proceeds, but in either case, the end result will be that a smaller number of machines will reach a given age would be the case if age or technical failure were the only source of obsolescence.

Let us denote the fraction of equipment which survives economically to age z as $\lambda_{p,z}$ and require that:

(2.1.67.) $$\lambda_{p,z} \leq l_{p,z} \quad , \quad \begin{array}{l} p = 1, \ldots, q \\ z = 1, \ldots, w \end{array}$$

Here again, the underlying assumption is that the development of a any vintage is a process which on average is described by the sequence of probabilites $\lambda_{p,z}$. Some units are scrapped before a given moment in time, others later; and on average $y_{p,t-z}\lambda_{p,z}$ machines will still be in use after z time steps. It does not seem to be possible to determine the economic loss rate $\lambda_{p,z}$ in a multi–sector model without prior knowledge of the system of prices[14]. Absent a proof of the contrary, this assertion in itself proves Robinson's (1954) claim that no capital aggregate can be formed which is independent of prices and profits. Finally, we introduce a measure that we shall need below, the life expectancy of a capital good of type p. Of the initial stock just finished, $y_{p,0}$, after z time steps still $y_{p,0} \cdot \lambda_{p,z}$ units are remain intact after z time steps, while after $z + 1$ time steps only $y_{p,0}l_{p,z+1}$ remain, and so on. Summation over all times up to the maximum lifetime w yields the total number of "machine hours" that a newly produced stock will ever perform:

$$\sum_{z=1}^{w} y_{p,0}l_{p,z}$$

We divide by the initial stock $y_{p,0}$ to find the average number of machine hours per unit of equipment $p, 0$ just finished, and this in turn gives its life expectancy $e_{p,0}$:

(2.1.68.) $$e_{p,0} = \frac{y_{p,0} \sum_{z=1}^{w} l_{p,z}}{y_{p,0}} = \sum_{z=1}^{w} l_{p,z}$$

The further life expectancy at age v of a capital good of type p is determined similarly:

$$\frac{\sum_{u=v+1}^{w} \text{stock } u}{\text{stock } v} = \frac{\text{initial stock} \cdot \sum_{u=v+1}^{w} l_u}{\text{initial stock} \cdot l_v}$$

---

[14] For a one–commodity system, see Solow et al. (1966).

that is,

$$(2.1.69.) \qquad e_{p,v} = \frac{\sum_{u=v+1}^{w} l_{p,u}}{l_{p,v}}$$

If the $l_{p,z}$ are replaced by $\lambda_{p,z}$, we obtain economic life expectancy rather than technical life expectancy. Since economic loss rates are never greater, and may well be less than technical loss rates, economic life expectancy is normally smaller than technical life expectancy.

Thus we have all the information we need to analyze the subsystem of capital goods. We have borrowed some ideas from demography to describe the state transitions within the stock of durable equipment, and we have related this stock to the flow system of production as well. In the end, we have seen that in general it is difficult to derive unambiguous results regarding the age composition of capital stocks, the aggregate technique of production, and the like. But many of the relations encountered here can be simplified and well defined solutions obtained if, as we shall do in the section which follows, the discussion is confined solely to steady states or, as the vocabulary of demography would have it, "stable populations".

2.1.2.2. Balanced Growth II: Accumulation of Durable Capital Goods

We turn now to an examination of balanced growth in an economy with durable capital goods. The problem here is to determine the warranted production rate of capital goods which suffices to both make up for the loss of equipment scrapped and to supply the means for further growth of productive capacity. As before, define α to be von Neumann's coefficient of expansion. In balanced growth, all quantities grow by this factor, as do the stocks of capital goods k_t, the inflows of equipment y_t, and losses $\delta_t k_t$:

$$(2.1.70.) \qquad k_{t+1} = \alpha k_t$$
$$(2.1.71.) \qquad y_{t+1} = \alpha y_t$$
$$(2.1.72.) \qquad \delta_{t+1} k_{t+1} = \alpha \delta_t k_t$$

Insertion of k_{t+1} into (2.1.72.) yields:

$$(2.1.73.) \qquad \delta_{t+1} \alpha k_t = \alpha \delta_t k_t$$

Dot multiplication by a vector $(\frac{1}{k_t})$ leads to:

$$(2.1.74.) \qquad \delta_{t+1} = \delta_t \quad ,$$

that is, given exponential growth or shrinkage the loss rates per time step must be constant for all capital goods. Such time invariance only exists if, first, all vintages of type $p, p = 1, \ldots, q$ in use conform to the same type–specific life table and, second, the age composition of all stocks remains constant. The first condition holds by assumption (no technical progress), the second is met if at least for w time steps investments have grown by the equilibrium rate α:

(2.1.75a.)
$$y_{p,t-z} = \alpha y_{p,t-z-1}$$

from which:

(2.1.75b.)
$$y_{p,t} = \alpha y_{p,t-1} = \alpha^2 y_{p,t-2} = \ \cdots \ = \alpha^w y_{p,t-w}$$

and:

(2.1.76.)
$$y_{p,t-z} = \alpha^{-z} y_{p,t}$$

This expression can be inserted into the equation which defines the present stock of type p, (2.1.41.):

(2.1.77.)
$$k_{p,t} = \sum_{z=1}^{w} \alpha^{-z} y_{p,t} \cdot l_{p,z} = y_{p,t} \sum_{z=1}^{w} \alpha^{-z} l_{p,z}$$

Thus, given a world of stable population, present capital stock may be calculated from present investment, the growth rate, and the set of survival probabilities; no knowledge of the past is necessary to determine events in the present.

Consider now the age composition of capital stocks. The mean age of equipment of type p, z_p, is a weighted average of all stocks of ages 0 through w which are in use at time t:

(2.1.78a.)
$$\bar{z}_p \quad = \quad \frac{y_{p,t} \sum_{z=1}^{w} z \alpha^{-z} l_{p,z}}{y_{p,t} \sum_{z=1}^{w} \alpha^{-z} l_{p,z}}$$

(2.1.78b.)
$$= \quad \frac{\sum_{z=1}^{w} z \alpha^{-z} l_{p,z}}{\sum_{z=1}^{w} \alpha^{-z} l_{p,z}}$$

Note that, because in a stable population of stocks the mean age is time invariant, (2.1.78b.) contains no time–dependent variables. This invariance, moreover, holds true for the ratio of the stocks of any two different vintages.

Let $u < w$ and $v < w$ be two distinct age cohorts or vintages of stocks of type p. Then:

$$(2.1.79.) \qquad \frac{y_{p,t-u}l_{p,u}}{y_{p,t-v}l_{p,v}} = \frac{y_{p,t}\alpha^{-u}l_{p,u}}{y_{p,t}\alpha^{-v}l_{p,v}} = \frac{\alpha^{-u}l_{p,u}}{\alpha^{-v}l_{p,v}}$$

Now the loss rate per time step is simply a cross–section through all the age cohorts of the stock. We have already determined $\delta_{p,t}$ to be:

$$(2.1.80.) \qquad \delta_{p,t} = \frac{1}{k_{p,t}} \sum_{z=1}^{w} y_{p,t-z}l_{p,z} \cdot m_{p,z+1}$$

Given stable population growth, (2.1.76.) and (2.1.77.) can be substituted for $y_{p,t-z}$ and $k_{p,t}$, respecively, so that:

$$(2.1.81.) \qquad \begin{aligned} \delta_p &= \frac{y_{p,t} \sum_{z=1}^{w} \alpha^{-z} l_{p,z} m_{p,z+1}}{y_{p,t} \sum_{z=1}^{w} \alpha^{-z} l_{p,z}} \\[2mm] &= \frac{\sum_{z=1}^{w} \alpha^{-z} l_{p,z} m_{p,z+1}}{\sum_{z=1}^{w} \alpha^{-z} l_{p,z}} \end{aligned}$$

determines the loss rate solely as a function of parameters. All of these properties, of course, are only valid where none of the growth or loss rates has been disturbed for at least w time steps, a condition which lies at the base of Lotka's (1939) theory of stable populations[15].

Once again, economic life tables can be inserted for the technical ones, so that the stock of equipment p is given by:

$$(2.1.77'.) \qquad k_{p,t} = y_{p,t} \sum_{z=1}^{w} \alpha^{-z} \lambda_{p,z}$$

Accordingly, the economic loss rate per time step is:

$$(2.1.80'.) \qquad \delta_p^{(\lambda)} = \frac{\sum_{z=1}^{w} \alpha^{-z} \lambda_{p,z} \mu_{p,z+1}}{\sum_{z=1}^{w} \alpha^{-z} \lambda_{p,z}}$$

where μ is the one–step probability of economic scrappage between the ages of z and $z + 1$. There is no clear relationship between the technical and economic loss rates.

---

[15] For a modern treatment of this field, see Keyfitz (1968).

Given the loss rates, the steady–state behavior of the production system is:

$$
\begin{array}{rcl}
(I - C)x_t &=& \alpha(Ax_t + My_t)\\
k_t &=& \alpha(Fx_t + Gy_t)\\
r_t &=& \alpha(Dx_t + Ny_t)\\
l_t &=& \alpha(Ex_t + Qy_t)\\
y_t &=& ((\alpha - 1)e + \delta) * k_t
\end{array}
$$

(2.1.82.)

where δ is the q–dimensional vector of time–invariant loss rates δ_p and e is the q–dimensional unit vector. Employing matrix notation, we can rearrange this system to yield:

(2.1.83.)
$$
\begin{pmatrix} (I-C)x \\ \frac{e}{(\alpha-1)e+\delta} * y \\ r \\ l \end{pmatrix}_t = \alpha \begin{bmatrix} A & M \\ F & G \\ D & N \\ E & Q \end{bmatrix} \begin{pmatrix} x \\ y \end{pmatrix}_t
$$

where the second element of the left–hand vector is a shorthand notation for:

(2.1.84.)
$$
\frac{e}{(\alpha - 1)e + \delta} * y_t = \begin{pmatrix} \frac{1}{\alpha-1+\delta_1} y_1 \\ \frac{1}{\alpha-1+\delta_2} y_2 \\ \vdots \\ \frac{1}{\alpha-1+\delta_q} y_q \end{pmatrix}_t
$$

Matrix [ ] of (2.1.83.) is not square, though the subsystem:

(2.1.85.)
$$
\begin{pmatrix} (I - C)x_t \\ \frac{e}{(\alpha-1)e+\delta} * y_t \end{pmatrix} = \alpha \begin{bmatrix} A & M \\ F & G \end{bmatrix} \begin{pmatrix} x \\ y \end{pmatrix}_t
$$

possesses a square matrix which is also indecomposable. That is, (2.1.85.) is the basic–commodity subsystem, and it can be solved by means of Frobenius' theorem. For this purpose, we define an auxiliary diagonal matrix whose first n elements are taken from $(I-C)$ and whose remaining q elements are drawn from vector (2.1.84.):

(2.1.86.)
$$
\begin{bmatrix}
1-\gamma_1 & & & & & & & 0 \\
& \ddots & & & & & & \\
& & 1-\gamma_n & & & & & \\
& & & \frac{1}{\alpha-1+\delta_1} & & & & \\
& & & & \frac{1}{\alpha-1+\delta_2} & & & \\
& & & & & \ddots & & \\
0 & & & & & & & \frac{1}{\alpha-1+\delta_q}
\end{bmatrix} := \Gamma
$$

Because $I - C \geq 0$ by assumption and $\alpha - 1 + \delta_p \geq 0$ for all p by (2.1.14.), Γ is always nonnegative. Γ will be strictly positive in its first n diagonal elements if no pure consumption goods exist, and will be strictly positive in its last q elements if gross investment is positive, that is, if α is exceeds the maximum possible rate of balanced decline $-\delta$. The system so defined:

$$(2.1.87.) \qquad \frac{1}{\alpha} \Gamma \begin{pmatrix} x \\ y \end{pmatrix} = \begin{bmatrix} A & M \\ F & G \end{bmatrix} \begin{pmatrix} x \\ y \end{pmatrix}$$

is an eigenvalue problem of the intermediate stage, see Collatz (1949). Given the additional restriction $\Gamma > 0$, it can be transformed into the special eigenvalue problem:

$$(2.1.88.) \qquad \Gamma^{-1} \begin{bmatrix} A & M \\ F & G \end{bmatrix} \begin{pmatrix} x \\ y \end{pmatrix} = \frac{1}{\alpha} \begin{pmatrix} x \\ y \end{pmatrix}$$

which possesses a positive solution vector with $1/\alpha$ as the maximum root of the left–hand matrix in (2.1.88.) (see Wielandt (1950)). Because each element of Γ^{-1} is the reciprocal of the corresponding element in Γ and is thus strictly positive, it is clear that Γ^{-1} will be positive if Γ is positive.

2.1.2.3. Observation Equations

Once again, a system of observation equations can be determined. We have:

$$(2.1.89.) \qquad \begin{pmatrix} (I - C)x \\ k \\ r \\ l \end{pmatrix} = \begin{bmatrix} \hat{A} & \hat{M} \\ \hat{F} & \hat{G} \\ \hat{D} & \hat{N} \\ \hat{E} & \hat{Q} \end{bmatrix} \begin{pmatrix} x \\ y \end{pmatrix}$$

such that:

$$(2.1.90.) \qquad \begin{pmatrix} \hat{A} \\ \hat{D} \\ \hat{E} \\ \hat{F} \\ \hat{G} \\ \hat{M} \\ \hat{N} \\ \hat{Q} \end{pmatrix} = \begin{pmatrix} A \\ D \\ E \\ F \\ G \\ M \\ N \\ Q \end{pmatrix}$$

There are observation equations as well for the composition of the stocks of equipment, that is, for the survival probabilities. Beginning with (2.1.77.), we have:

$$(2.1.91) \qquad l_{p,z} = \frac{k_{p,t,z}}{y_{p,t}} \alpha^z$$

An observation equation takes a growing system to be a stationary one, which means that the growth factor is neglected:

$$(2.1.92.) \qquad \hat{l}_{p,z} = \frac{k_{p,t,z}}{y_{p,t}} = \alpha^{-z} l_{p,z}$$

Using the same logic, stocks of different ages may be related to one another at the same time, that is, the average loss rate is evaluated by cross–section at time t rather than by comparison of stocks at times t and $t+1$. Thus, an observed measure of the loss rates is obtained:

$$
\begin{aligned}
\hat{\delta}_p &= \sum_{z=1}^{w} \frac{k_{p,t,z} - k_{p,t,z+1}}{k_{p,t,z}} \\
&= \sum_{z=1}^{w} \frac{(\alpha^{-z} l_{p,z} - \alpha^{-(z+1)} l_{p,z+1}) \cdot y_{p,t}}{\alpha^{-z} l_{p,z} \cdot y_{p,t}} \\
(2.1.93a.) \qquad &= \sum_{z=1}^{w} \frac{\hat{l}_{p,z} - \hat{l}_{p,z+1}}{\hat{l}_{p,z}}
\end{aligned}
$$

Closely related to this are the life expectancy and its observed value. The apparent life expectancy is found when all stocks in use are seen against the present output of capital goods:

$$\hat{e}_{p,0} = \sum_{z=1}^{w} \frac{k_{p,t,z}}{y_{p,t}} \qquad ,$$

which is equal to:

$$(2.1.93b.) \qquad \hat{e} = \sum_{z=1}^{w} \hat{l}_{p,z}$$

We have shown that under steady–state conditions the interrelations between the stock system and the flow system can be assumed away. This is so because (given α) gross investment y_p is a constant fraction of k_p, this is, the stocks of equipment of type p can be replaced by the flows of new capital goods of type p. We then obtained a system of commodity reproduction with $\begin{pmatrix} x \\ y \end{pmatrix}$ as the eigenvector and $\begin{bmatrix} r^{-1} & A & M \\ & F & G \end{bmatrix}$ as the matrix of input–output coefficients. This system has a positive eigenvector if its matrix of coefficients is both semipositive and indecomposable. In economic terms this implies that not only the commodity flows x are indispensible as inputs, but also that capital goods are basic products. Roughly this means that from the perspective of its total lifetime, each capital good is an indispensible (direct or indirect) input to all productions. However, this does not preclude that the same capital good is non–basic as seen from a given age z; only the weigthed sum of capital–input matrices must be indecomposable, none of the z–specific matrices needs to be indecomposable itself.

With the flows of capital goods being known, their respective stocks were easily calculated by (2.1.77.), and we obtained some simplified results on the observed stock/flow relationships. It must be remembered, however, that such solutions depend on the knowledge of the sequence of survival probabilities $l_{p,z}$. In general these depend on prices, and in Section 2.2.2. below we shall see that this imposes some additional restrictions on the solubility of the system.

Yet the system of economic quantities is not complete; an important case which we have omitted thus far is that of joint production. Since it is common practice of today to analyze capital goods within the framework of multi–product processes, the problem of joint production is of special interest here.

2.1.3. Joint Production

2.1.3.1. Production Equations

Thus far, it has been assumed that every production process results in but one output; so that each process could be unambiguously associated by index number with its product. The situation becomes more complicated, however, when we allow for the possibility of joint or combined production, in which several products may emerge from a single process and which thus requires that goods i, $i = 1, \ldots, m$, be clearly distinguished from production processes j, $j = 1, \ldots, m$ (see von Neumann (1937), Sraffa (1960)).

In practice, joint production is generally the rule, for in only a few production processes are there neither waste materials, exhaust gas, nor expended energy which must either be disposed of at some cost or, perhaps turned into commodities which might themselves be sold in markets. A special case of joint production is the use of capital goods. Like catalysts, they enter into the production process, act to increase its intensity, and then they emerge from it once again.

In this section, we begin by constructing the input–output form of the joint–production system, and then transform it into the state–space form. The intricacies involved with the introduction of durable capital goods are postponed until Section 3.2.

Let $z_j \geq 0$ be the intensity with which process j is conducted, measured in arbitrary units (typically the input or output of a characteristic factor or product). We now meet the convention that process intensities are related to the time at which the process is terminated. Toward this end, we define a_{ij} to be the input coefficient of commodity i per "intensity unit" of process j. As before, all intermediate goods are defined so as to correspond to the time pattern of one–step elementary processes. The total output of commodity i at time t is now given by the sum of the amounts produced in j processes:

$$(2.1.94.) \qquad x_{i,t} = \sum_{j=1}^{m} b_{ij} z_{j,t}$$

Those products which are not consumed enter into the processes beginning at time t:

$$(2.1.95.) \qquad (1 - \gamma_i) x_{i,t} = \sum_{j=1}^{m} a_{ij} z_{j,t+1}$$

Substituting, we obtain the division of good i into its various uses:

$$(2.1.96.) \qquad \sum_{j=1}^{m} b_{ij} z_{j,t} = \sum_{j=1}^{m} a_{ij} z_{j,t+1} + \gamma_{i,t} x_{i,t}$$

In equilibrium, with no more than $n < m$ processes in use, we have the n–dimensional system of equations:

$$(2.1.97.) \qquad B z_t = A z_{t+1} + C B z_t$$

with[16]:

$$(2.1.98.) \qquad c_t = C x_t = C B z_t$$

---

[16] On consumption in von Neumann models, see Morishima (1964) and, importantly, Morgenstern/Thompson (1967, 1976). Sraffa (1960) employs a model which is at least formally equivalent if $x_{t+1} = x_t$ that is, for stationary production. See Schefold (1980).

Process intensities are no illustrative concept. By inverting B the system is converted into its input–output form, that is, both inputs and outputs are measured in units of themselves, and the process intensities cancel out. Note that matrix B is always invertible; all n commodities are produced, and n processes are used. We have, first:

(2.1.99.)
$$z_t = B^{-1} x_t$$

and, after changing the time indices in (2.1.97.):

(2.1.100.)
$$x_t = AB^{-1} x_{t+1} + C x_t$$

For $x_{t+1} = x_t$, see Pasinetti (1980). This approach too has the form:

$$
\begin{aligned}
x_{t+1} &= \min\left(F x_t; G u_t\right) \\
y_t &= H x_t
\end{aligned}
$$

Here, must be assumed that A is invertible as well, that is, all commodities are used as intermediate inputs, and every process requires such inputs. Then:

(2.1.101.)
$$x_{t+1} = B \ A^{-1}(I - C) x_t$$

and we find:

(2.1.102.)
$$
\begin{array}{lcl lcl}
F &=& B \ A^{-1}(I - C) & u &=& r \\
G &=& D & y &=& c \\
H &=& C &&&
\end{array}
$$

The same system can be formed with intensities z as state variables. But the restriction that A is invertible is needed here as well. Neither in their reduced input–output form nor in the state–space form single–product systems may be empirically distinguished from joint–product systems.

2.1.3.2. Observation Equations

We now take a cross–section through system (2.1.97.). For the moment, we shall assume that process intensities are correctly observed, while the matrix A of input coefficients a_{ij} is related to process intensies at the starting time t rahter than the termination time $t + 1$. Then:

(2.1.103)
$$B z_t = \hat{A} z_t + B z_t$$

or, after substitution:

$$(2.1.104.) \qquad (I - C)x_t = \hat{A}z_t = \hat{A}B^{-1}z_t$$

The reverse form of bias occurs if we consider the intensities of processes $j, t+1$ which begin at time t instead of the activities which terminate at that time. Then:

$$(2.1.105.) \qquad \hat{B}z_{t+1} = Az_{t+1} + C\hat{B}z_{t+1} \quad , \quad x_t = \hat{B}z_{t+1}$$

and:

$$(2.1.106) \qquad (I - C)x_t = Az_{t+1} = A\hat{B}^{-1}z_{t+1}$$

A second approach is to proceed directly from the form of (2.1.100.). This is more plausible if process intensities are not observable but production flows are; a situation which is more likely than those considered above. We then have the observation equation:

$$(2.1.107.) \qquad x_t = \hat{A} \quad B^{-1}x_t$$

Note that in this form, input and output matrices themselves, and thus their observed values as well, cannot be distinguished empirically.

2.1.3.3. Balanced Growth III: Expansion of Process Intensities in von Neumann's Generalized Model

In joint production, balanced growth means that all process intensities expand at the same rate:

$$(2.1.108.) \qquad z_{t+1} = \alpha z_t \quad ,$$

where once again, α is von Neumann's proportionate factor of expansion. (2.1.97.) now becomes:

$$(2.1.109.) \qquad Bz_t = \alpha Az_t + CBz_t$$

or:

$$(2.1.110.) \qquad Cx_t = (B - \alpha A)z_t$$

59

and, after repeated substitution for Bz_t:

(2.1.111.) $$(I - C - \alpha AB^{-1})x_t = 0$$

The observation equation for the process intensities z is changed to:

(2.1.112.) $$(I - C)Bz_t = \hat{A}z_t = \alpha Az_t$$

Accordingly, the observation for the flow of intermediate goods becomes:

(2.1.113.) $$(I - C)x_t = \widetilde{AB}^{-1}x_t = \alpha AB_{-1}x_t$$

In this case, we have either $\hat{A} = \alpha A$ for B observable or $\widetilde{AB}^{-1} = \alpha AB^{-1}$ for B not observable.

2.1.4. Summary Remarks on Quantity Equations

In these sections on quantity equations, we have formalized some of the arguments presented verbally in Ch. 1. Assuming discrete time, it has been shown how multi–stage processes can be decomposed into elementary production steps, just as was proposed in the Lexis scheme framework of Chapter 1. Employing the elementary equations of motion of general systems theory, a difference–equation system of the material flow was constructed. What systems theory calls the state space is the commodity space in economic terms, where the state vector is interpreted as what economists call the output vector (this has a different meaning in systems theory). There is in economic input–output theory a class of models corresponding to this system, these are usually given in backward–recursive form. If all commodities are basic commodities (in the sense of their being indispensable), these backward–recursive models can be transformed into the forward–recursive state–space system. With non–basic commodities, subsystems are opened which cannot be put in the state–space form. But the behavior of these non–basic systems is determined by the underlying basic systems which can be written in either form without changing their character.

Along with each production system, there exists a system of observation equations. By observation we understand a cross–section through the equations of motion at a given moment in time and, unlike systems theory, concentrate our attention on the interrelations within the production sphere rather than on the relation between system inputs and system outputs, i.e. resources and consumer goods. It turns out that there are biases against the true flow coefficients; under steady–state conditions these biases are systematic. This sheds light on a class of input–output models which apply statics to dynamic structures. This problem shall be reconsidered in Sec. 3.1. below.

Particular complications are encountered when durable capital goods are taken into account. In economic theory, it is a well–established procedure to regard a capital good as a sequence of different goods which are distinct by age. This means to decompose stocks of commodities into flows of commodities which are treated as by–products to the output of intermediate products and consumer goods. In our view, it is a more obvious approach to regard the stocks of capital goods as a system of stocks, which is what we have attempted here. Formally, the stock system of capital goods is regarded as a population of as many genders as there are types of equipment manufactured, its state transition being described as a schedule of age–dependent patterns of obsolescence. We shall see in Section 2.2.2. below that this schedule is in fact dependent on prices, as is now conventional wisdom of capital theory. This system of stocks is related to the system of commodity flows by a system of capacity coefficients which indicate the number of pieces of equipment required per unit of output of intermediate goods; since durable means of production do not merge with products physically, no physical input coefficients can be defined. Rather, capital goods resemble catalysts which remain themselves unaffected by the processes in which they are required, and they are used up only to the extent in which they wear out after some time. The determination of wear and tear is itself an economic problem which can only be solved if prices and the rate of interest are known. Thus, it is a problem of price theory rather than of production theory to allocate the wear and tear of durables to the output of intermediate goods.

Under steady–state conditions, the formal description of the model with durables is simplified. As to the stock system, the equations describing the steady–state conditions are equivalent with some of the Lotka equations of stable–population theory; the age composition, the life expectancies, and so on, are all time invariant and depend solely on parameters. In the same manner, the observation equations of demography apply. With steady–state expansion, it is also possible to separate the system of flows from the stock system completely. We constructed a reduced system of quantities without stocks. Given the ratios of consumer demand to outputs, this system has a strictly positive eigenvector with the eigenvalue equal to the reciprocal of von Neumann's proportionate factor of expansion.

There is a class of still more general systems of production which exist in the form of joint–production models. These models assume that more than one kind of outputs emerge from a single process. This makes it necessary to conduct the analysis in terms of process levels rather than commodity outputs. We shortly presented this well–known problem and transformed the system into the state–space form. But since the resulting matrix of coefficients is not necessarily nonnegative, the Frobenius theorem cannot be applied. A special variant of joint–production theory is employed in capital theory. We shall evaluate our model in the light of that theory in Section 3.2. below. Before, we turn our attention to prices.

2.2. Price Equations

2.2.1. Price Formation without Durable Capital Goods

2.2.1.1. Price Equations

Everything has its price. In the analysis which follows, we shall assign a price $p_{i,t}$ to each commodity i at time t, whether there is actually a market price for that commodity or not. From the perspective of economic activity in the "real" world, the postulation of prices as ubiquitous as these is somewhat heroic, for it is scarcely possible to fix the going rate for goods, say an automobile body on a conveyor belt at the moment it is to be dipped into the paint bath, which are themselves never brought to market. As a result, many of the prices $p_{i,t}$ which we shall assign must be understood as mere accounting calculations or shadow prices.

Prices result from one another in much the same way as products emerge from one another. But because some time must elapse between the application of inputs to production and the sale of the finished goods which are ultimately produced, all production must in this sense be prefinanced. Interest charges thus insinuate themselves between input and output prices, that is, knowledge of the matrix of input coefficients does not suffice in itself to determine the structure of prices. This is in contrast to those theories of interest which are usually termed "neoclassical" and seek to explain also the rate of interest by the technical coefficients of production[1].

Formally, output prices are decomposed into the prices of commodity inputs and the prices of external inputs where they exist. From the point of view of system theory, this means that the state $p'^{(x)}$ of a price system is to be related both to the state of this system one time step earlier and to prices of resource inputs, $p'^{(r)}_t$. Let the state transition of this system be: $\tilde{F} : p \mapsto p$ and, similarly, let $\tilde{G} : r \mapsto p$ be the input functional. Then the following price system Π is obtained (Figure 24):

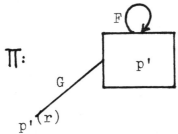

Fig. 24: Price System: State–Space Form

---

[1] See Lutz (1956) for a review, a critique of neoclassical approaches to the theory of interest is found in Hicks (1973).

Note that there are no outflows in this system; nothing which acts to diminish values is taken into account. Two problems present themselves for consideration. The first is to interpret the matrices $\tilde{F}$ and $\tilde{G}$ in economic terms, and the second is to determine the relationship between this system and the quantity systems of Section 2.1. above.

We examine first the way in which the price of commodiy i is formed. In order to produce one unit of i, inputs a_{ij} of commodities j, $j = 1, \ldots, n$, are required at time $t - 1$. Each of these intermediate inputs must be paid its price $p_{j,t-1}$ per unit, so that the total input cost per unit of output which results before production begins is given by:

$$
(2.2.1.) \qquad \frac{q^{(x)}_{i,t-1}}{x_{i,t}} = \sum_{j=1}^{n} p_{j,t-1} a_{ij}
$$

Accordingly, $x_i q^{(x)}_{i,t-1}$ is the amount industry i as a whole spends on the purchase of intermediate goods. In addition, it is possible that prices $p^{(r)}_k$ must be paid for the right to extract natural resources from the environment, that is, $p^{(r)}_k$ comprises possible rents. Resource costs per unit to be produced are thus:

$$
(2.2.2.) \qquad \frac{q^{(r)}_{i,t-1}}{x_{i,t}} = \sum_{k=1}^{m} p^{(r)}_{k,t-1} d_{ki}
$$

Similarly, human labor must be hired before production can begin. We assume that there are various kinds of human labor h, $h = 1, \ldots, l$ each of which commands a different wage w_h. Thus, wage costs incurred per unit of product are:

$$
(2.2.3.) \qquad \frac{q^{(l)}_{i,t-1}}{x_{i,t}} = \sum_{h=1}^{l} w_{h,t-1} e_{hi}
$$

In order to provide intermediate financing for all of these costs, investment funds, or capital, are required. Let us call investments in raw materials and intermediate products "circulating capital", and investments in wages or payroll the "wage fund". Together, these two elements form the working capital of industry i.

There is some ambiguity in economic theory as to whether wages and resource prices should be regarded as separate sources of value. Some deny that resources other than labor can be assigned values at all, while others claim that if labor commands a positive wage, it is for precisely the same reason that other resources are paid, their scarcity relative to demand. We take no position on this question here, for vectors of labor and other inputs are formally equivalent and we shall often neglect the possible difference between the two, although our franework allows such distinctions to be readily reintroduced.

Funds so invested at any point in time "work" in the production step which follows, and in general the proceeds from sales will not be the same as costs incurred, so profits or losses arise. The ratio of turnover to costs in production line i will be denoted $\beta_{i,t}$, such that after one time step:

(2.2.4.) $$p_{i,t} = \beta_{i,t} q_{i,t-1}$$

or, expanded in full:

(2.2.5.) $$p_{i,t} = \beta_{i,t} \sum_{j=1}^{n} p_{j,t-1} a_{ij} + \sum_{h=1}^{l} w_{h,t-1} e_{hi}$$

There are as many pricing equations as there are commodities, and in matrix notation, we have:

(2.2.6.) $$p't = \beta'_t(p'_{t-1}A + w'_{t-1}E)$$

Here, $\beta'_t = (\beta_1, \ldots, \beta_m)$ is a real n–dimensional real row vector, with the term $\beta'_t(\ )$ the dot product of vector β'_t and the row vector formed by the expression in brackets[2]. The typical element β_i of this vector or diagonal matrix represents the relative excess of returns over cost in production line i.

We have thus far assumed that human labor, like all other inputs, must be paid in advance. It thus appears that there is a wage capital upon which interest is charged. There is, however, a tradition extending back at least as far as Walras (1874) which denies the existence of such "wage funds" by assuming ex–post wage payments, and if this convention is adopted, price equation (2.2.6.) would become:

(2.2.7.) $$p'_t = (\beta'_t p'_{t-1} A) + w'^{(W)}_t E \qquad ,$$

where $w^{(W)}$ are Walrasian ex–post wages. Since wage payments now occur at the same moment as sales, there seems to be no need for wage funds. But

---

[2] β' may also be regarded as a diagonal matrix.

this is only a partial solution to the wage fund problem, for wage capital continues to exist even where wages are paid ex post, only its distribution is different, labor must simply prefinance itself. A worker given the choice of accepting either a Walrasian wage or a payment in advance will be indifferent between the two if the ex post wage just exceeds the advance wage by the interest rate on consumer credit:

(2.2.8.) $$w'^{(W)}_t = (1 + i_{t-1,t})w'_{t-1}$$

It may therefore be argued that ex post wages always include an element of interest, for they are in the the nature of a supplier's credit to the producer. As long as interest i represents the opportunity cost of investment to entrepreneurs as well, they too will be indifferent as to (2.2.8.).

Equation (2.2.7.) is also the state transition function of price system Π:

(2.2.9.) $$\Pi: \qquad p'_t = \beta' * (p'_{t-1}A + w'_{t-1}E)$$

where:

$$\tilde{F} = \beta' A \qquad \tilde{G} = \beta' E$$

and

$$w'_{t-1} \hat{=} p'^{(r)}_{t-1}$$

This last expression always holds true, for external inputs of any kind may be composed of either $p'^{(r)}$ or w. There is no problem in aggregating unit costs and revenues, for while apples cannot be compared to oranges, their prices can. The total working capital of industry i is denoted by its value W_i, and this is equal to the sum of costs incurred:

(2.2.10.) $$q_{i,t-1}x = W_{i,t-1}$$

Summing over all industries we obtain the economy's total working capital at time $t-1$, which is equal to the value of intermediate inputs plus the wage bill:

(2.2.11.) $$W_{t-1} = \sum_{i=1}^{n} q_{i,t-1}x_i = (p'_{t-1}A + w'_{t-1}E)x_t$$

Now consider the going rate of interest. Assume that there exists a current one-period loan rate $\iota_{t-1,t}$, which may be understood as a rate on call money. Further, let $\rho_{i,t}$ be the internal rate of return on capital in production line i, i.e.:

(2.2.12) $$\rho_{i,t} = \beta_{i,t} - 1$$

Then capital investment in production i yields an interest differential $\mu_{i,t}$:

(2.2.13.)
$$\mu_{i,t} = \rho_{i,t} - \iota_{t-1,t} \quad ,$$

and the internal rate of return may thus be represented as:

(2.2.14.)
$$\beta_{i,t} = 1 + \mu_{i,t} + \iota_{t-1,t}$$

Instant profitability requires at least that the interest differential not be negative[3].

The system of pricing equations is completed with the incorporation of price changes. Let ψ'_t be the $n-$ dimensional vector of price change factors $\psi_{i,t} \equiv p_{i,t}/p_{i,t-1}$. Then:

(2.2.15.)
$$p'_t = \psi'_t \cdot p'_{t-1}$$

Let $\pi_{i,t}$ be the rate of price change of good i from time $t-1$ to time t, so that ψ'_t is also given by:

(2.2.16.)
$$\psi'_t = (e' + \pi'_t) \quad ,$$

where e' is the $n-$dimensional unit row vector and π' is the vector of the rates of price change. Substitution into (2.2.6.) leads to:

(2.2.17.)
$$p'_{t-1}\psi'_t = \beta'_t \cdot p'_{t-1}A + \beta'_t \cdot w'_{t-1}E$$

2.2.1.2. Observation Equations

As we did earlier in the case of quantities, we now apply a cross–section to the Lexis scheme of prices. We assume first that matrices A and E are known and that there are difficulties only in observing prices. The observation equation which thus results is:

(2.2.18.)
$$p'_t = \hat{\beta}'_t(p'_t A + w'_t E)$$

Here, $\hat{\beta}'_t$ is the vector of interest factors measured by cross–section data:

(2.2.19.)
$$\hat{\beta}'_t = \frac{p'_t}{q'_t}$$

---

[3]On time profiles of investment, see however Hicks (1973).

The internal rates of return in cross–section are:

$$(2.2.20.) \qquad \hat{\rho}' = \frac{p'_t - q'_t}{q'_t}$$

From price equation (2.2.16.), one finds by "price adjustment":

$$(2.2.21a.) \qquad \hat{\rho}'_t = \frac{\beta'_{t+1}}{\psi'_{t+1}} q'_t$$

Substitution into observation (2.2.17.) yields:

$$(2.2.21b.) \qquad \hat{\beta}'_t = \frac{\beta'_{t+1}}{\psi'_{t+1}}$$

which means that by observing interest factors in cross–section data, price changes during the elementary production step are neglected. An additional complication arises when production coefficients are biased by observation as well. Then a modified observation equation is obtained in which:

$$(2.2.22.) \qquad p'_t = \hat{\beta}'_t (p'_t \hat{A} + w'_t \hat{E})$$

2.2.1.3. Uniform Rate of Profit I: Accumulation of Circulating Capital

Here, we investigate the special case in which all production lines yield the same profit. Then vector β'_t degenerates into a scalar $\beta^{(0)}$, which is von Neumann's interest factor. We assume further that all prices rise or fall by the same factor. Then there exists a scalar $\psi^{(0)}$ such that[4]:

$$(2.2.23.) \qquad p'_{t-1} \psi^{(0)} = \beta^{(0)} (p'_{t-1} A + w'_{t-1} E)$$

If a cross–section is applied to this system as well, and if technical coefficients are known, we have:

$$(2.2.24.) \qquad p'_t = \hat{\beta}^{(0)} (p'_t A + w'_t E)$$

Dividing pricing equation (2.2.23.) by $\psi^{(0)}$, we find:

$$(2.2.25.) \qquad p'_{t-1} = \frac{\hat{\beta}^{(0)}}{\hat{\psi}^{(0)}} (p'_{t-1} A + w'_{t-1} E)$$

---

[4] See Morishima (1964, p.137, (11)).

68

Substitution of (2.2.24.) yields:

$$(2.2.26.) \qquad \hat{\beta}^{(0)} = \frac{\beta^{(0)}}{\psi^{(0)}} \quad ,$$

that is, the bias in observing the interest factor is equal to the overall rate of price change. This conveys a piece of important information, namely that the observed internal rate of return $\hat{\rho}^{(0)} \equiv \hat{\beta}^{(0)} - 1$ is just Fisher's (1930) real rate of interest:

$$\begin{aligned} \hat{\beta}^{(0)} \quad &= \quad 1 + \hat{\rho}^{(0)} \quad = \quad \tfrac{1+\rho^{(0)}}{1+\pi^{(0)}} \quad ; \\ 1 + \rho^{(0)} \quad &= \quad (1 + \hat{\rho}^{(0)})(1 + \pi^{(0)}) \quad = \\ &= \quad 1 + \hat{\rho}^{(0)} + \pi^{(0)} + \hat{\rho}^{(0)}\pi^{(0)} \quad ; \end{aligned}$$

$$(2.2.27.) \qquad \hat{\rho}^{(0)} = \rho^{(0)} - \pi^{(0)} - \hat{\rho}^{(0)}\pi^{(0)}$$

We now make the additional assumption that the economy expands by factor α and that matrices A and E are unknown. Then observation equation (2.2.22.) becomes:

$$\begin{aligned} p_t' = \hat{\hat{\beta}}^{(0)} (p_t'\hat{A} + w_t'\hat{E}) \\ (2.2.28.) \qquad = \hat{\hat{\beta}}^{(0)} \alpha(p_t'A + w_t'E) \end{aligned}$$

Equating this to (2.2.3.) yields:

$$(2.2.29.) \qquad \hat{\hat{\beta}}^{(0)} = \frac{1}{\alpha}\hat{\beta}^{(0)}$$

Compared to its true value $\beta^{(0)}$, the observed interest factor $\hat{\beta}^{(0)}$ is biased (or, more precisely, adjusted) by prices, whereas the observation $\hat{\hat{\beta}}^{(0)}$ is additionally biased by the growth factor α.

It may again be asked whether there are solutions to the system. But without further restrictive assumptions it seems hopeless to look for a solution to the general system:

$$(2.2.6.) \qquad p_t' = \beta'(p_{t-1}'A + w_{t-1}'E)$$

The most that can be said is that the passage of time always imposes histori-cal solutions on this equation. Price observation, coupled with the confidence that observed prices are good estimators for prices in the near future, is thus not an unreasonable method of price determination.

Of course, solutions do exist for stationary price systems (indeed this, and only this, is the domain of economic price theory). Assume now that quantities grow by α. We have seen that the system:

$$x_t = \alpha A x_t + C x_t$$

(with A and C semipositice and A indecomposable) has an eigenvector x which is strictly positive. From the existence of a positive vector x follows the existence of a dual vector $y > 0$ which, like x, is determined up to a multiple λ:[5]

(2.2.30.) $$y' = \alpha y' A + y' C$$

i.e. of a positive price vector:

(2.2.31.) $$p' = \alpha p' A + p' C$$

Note that with matrices A and C known, relative prices are determined, independently of wages and profits! Indeed there is a degree of freedom here. The associated cost–of–production equation, assuming constant prices, is:

(2.2.23.) $$p' = \beta p' A + \beta w' E$$

The price equation obtained by duality:

$$p' = \alpha p' A + p' C$$

is clearly not the equation desired, for it includes α rather than the interest factor β_ρ and per–unit output of consumption goods rather than per–unit input of wage costs ex post. An immediate solution exists if $\alpha \overset{!}{=} \beta$. Then:

(2.2.32.) $$p' C \overset{!}{=} \alpha w' E$$

---

[5] On such duality in economic production systems see, for example, Nikaidô (1968), Rockafellar (1974). A textbook treatment in the context of linear dynamic systems is Luenberger (1979). The locus classicus of duality between growth rates and profit rates is, of course, von Neumann (1937).

But unit consumption is often greater or smaller than ex–post wage cost evaluated at $\beta = \alpha$:

$$(2.2.33.) \qquad\qquad p'C \;\underset{>}{\overset{<}{}}\; \alpha w'E$$

If it is greater than the optimal ex–post wage cost, the interest factor exceeds α, and conversely. Let this difference in value be $p'U$, so that:

$$(2.2.34.) \qquad\qquad p' = \beta p'A + \beta w'E = \alpha p'A + \alpha w'E + p'U$$

We may plausibly interpret $p'U$ as per–unit net consumption out of profits, though this is somewhat inexact[6]. Solving for $p'U$, we find:

$$(2.2.35.) \qquad\qquad p'U = (\beta - \alpha)(p'A + w'E)$$

It is clear from (2.2.22.) that:

$$(2.2.36.) \qquad\qquad p'A + w'E = \frac{1}{\beta}p'$$

and thus U is found to be a scalar such that:

$$(2.2.36.) \qquad\qquad p'U = \frac{\beta - \alpha}{\beta}p'$$

We can now see that, with p' and α given from (2.2.31.), there will always exist infinitely many combinations of β and w' such that:

$$(2.2.37.) \qquad\qquad p^{*\prime} = \beta(p^{*\prime}A + w'E)$$

The duality employed here is interesting also from the system–theoretic perspective of Section 2.1.,since the price system in (forward–recursive) state–space form is the dual to the quantity system in backward–recursive input–output form. Illustrated graphically, this becomes:

---

[6] In the literature on duality in Sraffa/von Neumann systems with consumption, it is usual to define an aggregate commodity Vx whose value is equal to the wage bill. This composite commodity is then understood as workers' consumption. See, for example, Morishima (1973). But this interpretation is not necessary, for the definition provides no information on the class–specific ratios of consumption to income. Similarly, our composite commodity Ux is just the excess of total comsumption over the wage bill. See Mainwaring (1982) and the reply of Fujimoto (1983) for recent discussions in this field.

71

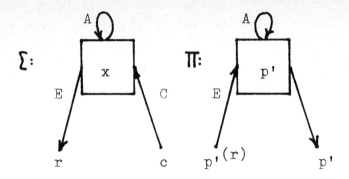

a) Backward–Recursive Quantity System b) Forward–Recursive Price System

Fig. 25: Duality between Prices and Production

Observe that the price system employs the same mappings as the quantity system, with just the direction of the arrows reversed. What appear as "outputs" to the backward–recursive quantity system, the external inputs r, are now the inputs to the forward–recursive price system, now shaped as input prices $p'^{(r)}$. Similarly c, the "input" to the quantity system, becomes output in the price system. There is, of course, a duality between consumption and external inputs, we have seen above that their values are equal in the state of optimum growth. In the same way, the growth factor α and the interest factor β are dual to one another.

There remains the further problem of finding the suitable vector of wage rates. It is clear that (2.2.22.) has no general solution in w, for:

$$(2.2.38.) \qquad w'E = \frac{1}{\beta}p'(I - \beta A)$$

where E is not invertible. This problem is familiar in both Walrasian theory and the labor theory of value (see, for example, Dorfman/Samuelson/Solow (1958)), and there are two paths which might be taken in adressing it. On the one hand, we may assume that that there are as many resources as there are finished goods and that there is no circulating capital; this is the Walrasian approach. On the other, we may assume that there is but one kind of external input, namely homogenous labor. In this latter case e is a vector now and w a scalar. Then:

$$(2.2.39.) \qquad p' = \beta(p'A + we')$$

and:

$$(2.2.40.) \qquad e' = \frac{1}{\beta w}p'(I - \beta A)$$

From this, the so-called wage–interest relation is given by:

$$(2.2.41.) \qquad de = 0 = \frac{\partial \frac{1}{\beta w}}{\partial w} dw + \frac{\partial \frac{1}{\beta w}}{\partial \beta} d\beta + \frac{1}{\beta w} \frac{\partial p'(I - \beta A)}{\partial \beta} d\beta$$

from which, for any given p':

$$(2.2.42.) \qquad \frac{dw}{d\beta} = -\frac{e'}{\beta w^2 p'} < 0 \qquad \text{if} \quad \beta > 0$$

This means that for one kind of labor, there are infinitely many combinations of w and β which correspond to (2.1.37.).

The results obtained here point to an interesting problem in Austrian cost theory (which in fact goes back to early criticism of Ricardo). Following Menger (1871), Austrian theory claims that prices are mainly determined by the demand for consumer goods and derived demands for goods of higher order, rather than by rents, the division of income or the like. Ricardian theory, in contrast, maintains that prices are determined from the input side if the wage rate (or, in neo-Ricardian analysis, the profit rate) is known. This, however, does not necessarily entail a contradiction. In equilibrium, prices can be determined as a dual to a given system of quantities, given that consumer demand Cx and investor demand Ax_{t+1} are known, see (2.2.31.). Then input prices are irrelevant, this is, so to speak, the Austrian view[7].

But the same is true if prices are determined on the cost side. Solve (2.2.40.) for p'_t to find:

$$(2.2.43.) \qquad p'_t = \beta w e'(I - \beta A)^{-1}$$

This yields equilibrium prices $p^{*'}$ with quantities made irrelevant; this is the Ricardian side of the coin (see also Arrow/Starrett (1971)). Both views are

---

[7]It should be noted that this interpretation is incorrect from a historical point of view. The older Austrian theory regarded production as a one–way process from primary inputs to consumer goods. In terms of matrix A, this implies that only the upper–diagonal elements $a_{i,i+1}$ are positive while all others fall to zero. It is clear that in this case, no self–sustained solution to the demand–sided price system (2.2.31.) exists. It is a strange corollary indeed that the Austrian problem of price determination is only soluable if loops ("*Rückversetzung*") are introduced in the chain of production! On modern discussions of Austrian theory, see, for example, Orosel (1979, 1980), Faber (1979) or Reiss (1980).

correct in equilibrium, and both concepts are of only limited use outside of it.

To achieve more generality in our results, durable means of production have to be included in the analysis, a task to which we now turn.

2.2.2. Price Formation with Durable Capital Goods

2.2.2.1. Price Equations

When capital goods are taken into consideration, price equations become more complex, for prices of producers' goods, investment goods and used equipment must be formed simultaneously. There is a dispute of long standing as to just what constitutes the proper approach to the theory of prices with durable capital. At the moment the joint–production method seems to have gained ground even outside the Sraffa School[8], but as was the case in the discussion of the quantity system, we shall not follow this approach. Instead, it will be tried to reach the same results in a slightly different way, and in Section Ch. 3.2., we shall demonstrate that both methods are feasible and that each can be transformed into the other[9].

There are related attempts to analyze a capital–stock subsystem such that equivalence with Sraffa's (1960) method is assured, see, for example, Jaksch (1975), Orosel (1977). But these systems suffer from the fact that the life table of durable stocks is fixed exogenously. Moreover, these attempts fail to introduce age–specific techniques of production. An older machine tool, for example, may be still quite helpful in cutting raw–metal lumps, although it is less valuable in working precise metal parts. This implies for an aging capital good that its destination in production changes, and hence capital theory must take into account that the technical performance of capital goods varies with increasing age.

We turn first to the prices of used capital goods. Let $p_{p,t,z}^{(k)}$ be the unit price paid at time t for equipment of type p and age z. Between the ages z and $z+1$ the capital good undergoes a change in value: on the one hand, its maximum future lifetime is diminished, lowering its value, but at the same time its survival of an age–specific loss risk bestows an additional future lifetime upon it, which tends to raise its value. The locus of such price

---

[8] See, for example, Hicks (1973), Burmeister (1974), Morishima (1973) and Morishima/Catephores (1978), Samuelson (1985).

[9] However, it should be noted that both the line of reasoning and the principal results presented here are borrowed from Schefold's (1979) analysis of capital goods in the context of joint production.

change is the production of commodities x and y. All capital goods are used in production; we have previously denoted this as:

$$(2.1.55.) \qquad k_t = Fx_{t+1} + Gy_{t+1}$$

Consider now a market for used equipment where producers have the choice of either renting capital goods or purchasing them before production and reselling them afterwards. For any such leasing, a rental or user price $p_{p,t}^{(u)}$, which in equilibrium reimburses owners for both the market rate of interest and the amortization of equipment, is charged. The price system now include prices for producers' goods $p'^{(x)}$, for investment goods $p'^{(y)}$, and for rentals $p'^{(u)}$, all of which are connected to one another by technical input coefficients:

$$(2.2.44a.) \qquad p'^{(x)} = \beta'^{(x)}(p'^{(x)}_{t-1}A + p'^{(u)}_{t-1}F + w'_{t-1}E)$$
$$(2.2.44b.) \qquad p'^{(y)} = \beta'^{(y)}(p'^{(x)}_{t-1}M + p'^{(u)}_{t-1}G + w'_{t-1}Q)$$

where once again the vector w' may be thought of as comprising both wages paid to labor and resource prices. Given age–dependent techniques, user prices $p'^{(u)}_z$ are in general not equal, or different profits would accrue. We shall examine this problem presently.

The alternative to leasing equipment is the purchase of machines before production and their subsequent resale. Here, the purchase price is the going price at time t for used machinery of age z and type p, $p_{p,t,z}^{(k)}$. The resale prise is the market price of $z+1$–old equipment one time step later, or $p_{p,t+1,z+1}^{(k)}$.

A fraction $m_{z+1} = (m_{1,z+1} \ldots m_{q,z+1})'$ of each vintage z fails physically between two successive moments in time:

$$(2.1.42.) \qquad k_{t-1,z} = k_{t,z+1} + m_{z+1} \cdot k_{t-1,z}$$

Accordingly, of each type the fraction $1 - m_{p,z+1}$ survives from age z to age $z + 1$. We denote these one–period rates of survival as a diagonal matrix

$$T_{z+1} = \begin{bmatrix} 1 - m_{1,z+1} & & \\ & \ldots & \\ & & 1 - m_{q,z+1} \end{bmatrix}.$$ Capital goods $k_{t-1,z}$ enter into

production as determined by F_z and G_z, and after production they reappear in the same proportions, diminished by physical losses[10]. Thus (see also

---

[10] Machines, of course, are not deflating balloons; this property refers only to the age cohort as a whole. Note that such cohort analysis of durable stocks is a macroeconomic concept.

(2.1.47b.) above):

$$(2.2.45.) \quad F_z x_{t,z} + G_z y_{t,z} = \underbrace{T_{z+1}(F_z x_{t,z} + G_z y_{t,z})}_{k_{t,z+1}}$$

$$+ \ (I - T_{z+1})(F_z x_{t,z} + G_z y_{t,z})$$

Price equations (2.2.44.) thus become[11]:

$$(2.2.46a.) \quad \beta'^{(x)} * (p'^{(x)}_{t-1}A + p'^{(k)}_{t-1}F + w'_{t-1}E)_z = p'^{(x)}_t + p'^{(k)}_{t,z+1}T_{z+1}F_z$$

$$(2.2.46b.) \quad \beta'^{(y)} * (p'^{(x)}_{t-1}M + p'^{(k)}_{t-1}G + w'_{t-1}Q)_z = p'^{(y)}_t + p'^{(k)}_{t,z+1}T_{z+1}G_z$$

In the case in which the options of leasing or purchase–resale are equally profitable, it must be true that:

$$(2.2.47a.) \quad p'^{(u)}_{t-1,z}F_z x_z = p'^{(k)}_{t-1,z}F_z x_z - \frac{1}{\beta}p'^{(k)}_{t,z+1}T_{z+1}F_z x_z$$

$$(2.2.47b.) \quad p'^{(u)}_{t-1,z}G_z y_z = p'^{(k)}_{t-1,z},G_z y_z - \frac{1}{\beta}p'^{(k)}_{t-1,z+1}T_{z+1}G_z y_z$$

Omitting some of the z–indices, this can be combined to yield:

$$(2.2.48.) \quad p'^{(u)}_{t-1}(FG)\begin{pmatrix} x \\ y \end{pmatrix} = p'^{(k)}_{t-1,z}(FG)\begin{pmatrix} x \\ y \end{pmatrix} - \frac{1}{\beta}p'^{(k)}_{t,z+1}T_{z+1}(FG)\begin{pmatrix} x \\ y \end{pmatrix}$$

Expression $(FG)\begin{pmatrix} x \\ y \end{pmatrix}$ may be replaced by its left–hand side $k_{t-1,z}$:

$$(2.2.49.) \quad p'^{(u)}_{t-1,z}k_{t-1,z} = p'^{(k)}_{t-1,z} - \frac{1}{\beta}p'^{(k)}_{t,z+1}T_{z+1}k_{t-1,z}$$

From Section 2.2 it is known that for all capital goods:

$$(2.1.42.') \quad k_{p,t-1,z} = (1 - m_{p,z+1})k_{p,t-1,z} + m_{p,z+1}k_{p,t-1,z}$$

[11] The following step is closely analogous to the joint–production approach, save for the fact that no output matrix is needed here. See also Section 3.2. below.

76

Equation (2.2.49.) is therefore valid for every element of vector k. The system may thus be dot–multiplied by $\frac{1}{k}$, and if scrappage prices are assumed to be zero and time indices changed, we find:

$$(2.2.50.) \qquad p'^{(u)}_{t,z} = p'^{(k)}_{t,z} - \frac{1}{\beta} p'^{(k)}_{t,z+1} T_{z+1}$$

This means that the price vector of stocks of age z is composed of today's rentals plus the stock prices of the subsequent point in time, the latter weighted by the one–period survival probabilites and the discount factor:

$$(2.2.51.) \qquad p'^{(k)}_{t,z} = p'^{(u)}_{t,z} + \frac{1}{\beta} p'^{(k)}_{t+1,z+1} \times T_{z+1} = p'^{(u)}_{t,z} + \frac{1}{\beta} p'^{(k)}_{t+1,z+1} * \frac{l'_{z+1}}{l'_z}$$

Successive replacement of future stock prices by rentals yields:

$$(2.2.52.) \qquad p'^{(k)}_{t,z} = \sum_{v=1}^{w-z} \beta^{-v}_{t+v} p'^{(u)}_{t+v,z+v} * \frac{l'_{z+v}}{l'_z}$$

Here the right-hand side is equal to the further life expectancy l'_{z+v}/l'_z, weighted by future rentals of surviving machines and by discount factors.

The price of a new machine remains to be determined. Due to the time structure of investment, machinery finished today will not add to productive capacity before tomorrow:

$$(2.1.53.) \qquad y_t = k_{t+1} - (e - \delta_t) * k_t$$

which implies that new equipment is 'stored' for one period before it yields returns. Taking storage within process z as an example, we find:

$$(2.2.53.) \quad \beta(p'^{(x)} A + p'^{(k)}_z F + w' E + p'^{(y)})_{t,z}$$
$$= p'^{(x)}_{t+1} + [p'^{(k)}_{t+1,z+1} T_{z+1}] F_z + p'^{(k)}_{t+1,1} T_1$$

from which, by application of (2.2.46a.):

$$(2.2.54.) \qquad \beta p'^{(y)}_t = p'^{(k)}_{t+1,1}$$

Here we have once more assumed $m_1 = 0$, i.e. $T_1 = I$; all new equipment arrives at the user's premises without loss in transit. This completes the induction, and by substituting $p'^{(y)}$ into (2.2.52.), we find:

$$(2.2.55.) \qquad p'^{(y)}_t = \sum_{z=1}^{w} p'^{(k)}_{t+z,z} \beta^{-z}_{t+z} * l'_z \quad , \quad l'_1 = e$$

that is, that the sales price of new equipment is equal to its expected return. Note that this equality has not been imposed as a restriction. Rather, it is a consequence from the uniform profit rate which characterizes (2.2.47.). This is what distinguishes our approach from the method employed by Arrow (1964), Hall (1968) and Jorgenson (1973, 1980) who follow Hotelling (1925) in restricting the price of new equipment to the present value of its earnings. The main implication of this difference is that in our framework, commodity prices are needed to determine the prices of capital services, not the other way round. This also has consequences for the validity of the Walrasian system, a problem that will be examined further in Chapter 3 below.

It need not be the case that hiring and purchasing capital goods are equally profitable. If they are not, prices $p'^{(y)}$ do not reflect the present value of rental payments, and (2.2.55.) becomes:

$$(2.2.56.) \qquad p'^{(y)}_t = \varepsilon' \sum_{z=1}^{w} p'^{(u)}_{t+z,z} \beta^{-z}_{t+z} l'_z$$

where ε' is a multiplicative measure of the capital value of investment in durable capital goods. The p–th capital value is negative if ε' exceeds unity and vice versa.

Before examining steady–state solutions to the price system, we turn to the observation equations.

2.2.2.2. Observation Equations

Once again, a cross–section may be passed through the cost–of–production equations (2.2.44.):

$$(2.2.57a.) \qquad p'^{(x)}_t = \hat{\beta}'^{(x)}_t (p'^{(x)}_t A + p'^{(u)}_t F + w'_t E)$$

$$(2.2.57b.) \qquad p'^{(y)}_t = \hat{\beta}'^{(y)}_t (p'^{(x)}_t M + p'^{(u)}_t G + w'_t Q)$$

There is similarly an observation equation for the price relations of stocks of two different age cohorts. Here, we relate today's stock of age z to today's stock of age $z + 1$, both at current prices:

$$(2.2.58.) \qquad p'^{(k)}_{t,z} = \hat{\varepsilon}'_z p'^{(u)}_{t,z} + \beta'^{-1}_t \, p'^{(k)}_{t,z+1} \frac{y'_{t-z-1} l'_{z+1}}{y'_{t-z} l'_z}$$

An observation of such kind also exists for the prices of new investment goods:

$$(2.2.59.) \qquad p'^{(y)} = \hat{\varepsilon}'_z \frac{p'^{(u)}_t \sum_{z=1}^{w} y'_{t-z} \cdot l'_z \beta'^{-z}}{y'_t}$$

78

or, more naively, neglecting interest:

$$(2.2.60.) \qquad p'^{(y)}_t = \hat{\bar{\varepsilon}}' \cdot \frac{p'^{(u)}_t \cdot k'_t}{y'_t} = \hat{\bar{\varepsilon}}' p'^{(u)}_t \cdot \hat{e}'_0$$

with $\hat{e}'_0$ the observed value of the life expectancy of new equipment and $\hat{\bar{\varepsilon}}'$ the price–deflated and interest–biased estimator for the disutility of investment.

2.2.2.3. Uniform Rate of Profit II: Accumulation of Fixed Capital

Given a uniform rate of profit and quasi–stationary prices, the pricing equations are simplified, in that vector β' degenerates into a uniform interest factor $\beta^{(0)}$ and vector ψ' of eigenrates of interest collapses into a uniform price inflator $\psi^{(0)}$. We assume further that all physical outputs grow by factor α, as was described in Section 2.1. above. Then there are $n + q$ quasi–stationary equations which determine costs of production as:

$$(2.2.61a.) \qquad \psi^{(0)} p'^{(x)}_{t-1} = \beta^{(0)}(p'^{(x)}_{t-1} A + p'^{(u)}_{t-1} F + w'_{t-1} E)$$

$$(2.2.61b.) \qquad \psi^{(0)} p'^{(y)}_{t-1} = \beta^{(0)}(p'^{(x)}_{t-1} M + p'^{(u)}_{t-1} G + w'_{t-1} Q)$$

Given these restrictions, there do exist equilibrium solutions to the price system. In (2.2.61.), all prices are expressed in terms of prices at time $t - 1$, so we might omit time indices. Dividing $\beta^{(0)}$ by $\psi^{(0)}$, we obtain a real rate of interest. Let the deflated interest factor be β_ρ. If vector $p'^{(u)}$ were known, prices $p'^{(x)}$ and $p'^{(y)}$ could be determined straightaway. But these prices are themselves required to determine the sequence of $p'^{(u)}_z$; the rental for capital goods is equal to the difference between the revenues from sales and cost–plus–interest. A way must therefore be found to determine costs and returns without employing rentals. A method proposed by Sraffa (1960) is to construct a reduced price system in which rentals on capital etc. are cancelled out. Consider a vintage of capital goods $k_{t,z}$. If this vintage is followed over its entire lifetime, it is seen to enter and emerge from processes $s \leq w$ times, where s is its maximum lifetime. Before entering the first process, it bears the unit prices of newly produced goods, and after it emerges from the last of the processes, its value has disappeared entirely. During its lifetime, the equipment consumes certain amounts of inputs and produces corresponding quantites of output. An obvious procedure is to aggregate all of these inputs and outputs into a single integrated process of duration s. Then all used machinery cancels out, and the total value created is just the discounted returns from inputs and outputs of commodities x,y. Beginnig with process 1, we find:

$$\beta\left((p'^{(x)}p'^{(k)})\begin{bmatrix} A & M \\ F & G \end{bmatrix} + w'(EQ)\right)_1 \binom{x}{y}_1 =$$

$$= (p'^{(x)}p'^{(y)} + p'^{(k)}_2 T_2(FG)_1)\binom{x}{y}_1$$

(2.2.62.)
$$\beta\left((p'^{(x)}p'^{(k)})\begin{bmatrix} A & M \\ F & G \end{bmatrix} + w'(EQ)\right)_2 \binom{x}{y}_2 =$$

$$= (p'^{(x)}p'^{(y)} + p'^{(k)}_3 T_3(FG)_2)\binom{x}{y}_2$$

$$\vdots$$

$$\beta\left((p'^{(x)}p'^{(k)})\begin{bmatrix} A & M \\ F & G \end{bmatrix} + w'(EQ)\right)_w \binom{x}{y}_w = (p'^{(x)}p'^{(y)})\binom{x}{y}_w$$

If quantities produced by capital goods of age z, $\binom{x}{y}_z$, conform to equilibrium, that is, if:

$$k_1 = (FG)_1 \binom{x}{y}_1$$

$$\frac{l_2}{l_1} * k_1 = T_2 k_1 = k_2 = (FG)_2 \binom{x}{y}_2$$

(2.2.63.)
$$\vdots$$

$$\frac{l_w}{l_1} * k_1 = \prod_{i=1}^{w} T_i k_1 = k_w = (FG)_w \binom{x}{y}_w$$

then the capital goods output of process z is equal to the corresponding input of process $z + 1$, and we may write:

(2.2.64.)
$$p'^{(k)}_{z+1} T_{z+1}(FG)_z = p'^{(k)}_{z+1}(FG)_{z+1}$$

If now processes are discounted by β^{-z}, we find for processes z and $z+1$:

$$
\text{(2.2.65a.)} \quad \beta^{-z+1}\left((p'^{(x)}p'^{(k)})\begin{bmatrix} A & M \\ F & G \end{bmatrix} + w'(EQ)\right)_z
$$

$$
= \beta^{-z}(p'^{(x)}p'^{(y)}) + \beta^{-z}p'^{(k)}_{z+1}T_{z+1}(FG)_z
$$

$$
\text{(2.2.65b.)} \quad \beta^{-z}\left((p'^{(x)}p'^{(k)})\begin{bmatrix} A & M \\ F & G \end{bmatrix} + w'(EQ)\right)_{z+1}
$$

$$
= \beta^{-(z+1)}(p'^{(x)}p'^{(y)}) + \beta^{-z+1}p'^{(k)}_{z+2}T_{z+2}(FG)_{z+1}
$$

In summing up, all terms in $p'^{(k)}$ cancel out. For example, in (2.2.65.):

$$
\text{(2.2.66.)} \quad \beta^{-z}p'^{(k)}_{z+1}T_{z+1}(FG)_z = \beta^{-z}p'^{(k)}_{z+1}(FG)_{z+1}
$$

Here, the left–hand side is equal to the second term on the right–hand side of (2.2.65a.), and the right–hand side equals capital goods inputs on the left–hand side of (2.2.65b.). There is an initial process where capital goods enter production for the first time. Capital goods entering productive capacity are one period old at least and have prices $\beta p'^{(y)}$, so:

$$
\text{(2.2.67.)} \quad \beta\left((p'^{(x)}\beta p'^{(y)})\begin{bmatrix} A & M \\ F & G \end{bmatrix} + w'(EQ)\right)_1 =
$$

$$
= (p'^{(x)}p'^{(y)}) + p'^{(k)}_1 T_2(FG)_1
$$

There is no counterpart for $\beta p'^{(y)}(FG)_1$ which removes it from the calculation, so it is preserved in the reduced system of prices:

$$
\text{(2.2.68.)} \quad \beta\left((p'^{(x)}p'^{(y)})\begin{bmatrix} \tilde{A} & \tilde{M} \\ \tilde{F} & \tilde{G} \end{bmatrix} + w'(\tilde{E}\tilde{Q})\right) = (p'^{(x)}p'^{(y)})
$$

where:

$$
\text{(2.2.69.)} \quad \begin{array}{ll} \tilde{a}_{ij} = \sum_{z=1}^{w} \beta^{-z}a_{ij,z} & \tilde{m}_{ip} = \sum_{z=1}^{w} \beta^{-z}m_{ip,z} \\ \tilde{f}_{pq} = f_{pq,1} & \tilde{g}_{pq} = g_{pq,1} \end{array}
$$

If we ignore the problem of how the vector of wage rates is to be determined, this system can be solved using the theorem of Frobenius. With the prices thus obtained, the user costs of durable goods may now be determined. The user cost of machinery of age z is equal to revenues minus the ex–post values of commodity inputs and wages, see (3.2.61.). If this equation is solved for user costs $p'^{(u)}_z$, a fine point emerges. Matrix FG is a $q \times n + q$–matrix and as such is not invertible:

$$(2.2.70.) \qquad p'^{(u)}(FG) = \frac{1}{\beta_\rho}(p'^{(z)}p'^{(y)}) - p'^{(z)}(AM) - w'(EQ)$$

A solution must therefore be sought in the subsystem of capital–goods production. If matrix G is invertible, we find:

$$(2.2.71.) \qquad p'^{(u)}_z = (\beta_\rho^{-1}p'^{(y)} - p'^{(z)}M_z - w'Q_z)G_z^{-1}$$

There are several conclusions to be drawn from this result. First, if a solution to the problem of user costs of durable equipment exists at all, it is to be found in the reproduction of capital goods and nowhere else, a point which recalls Marxist notions of the reproduction process. Second, for a solution to exist it is required that durable means of production must themselves be basic commodities in the manufacture of capital goods. Finally, there are $s \le w$ equations like (2.2.71.) which exist alongside one another and determine the user cost of equipment at every age up to s, and there is no reason for all of these prices to be positive. If, for a certain type of machinery, its market price $p^{(k)}_{p,v}$ falls to zero at age $v < s$, the equipment is scrapped, regardless of its possible further technical life expectancy; for the disappearance of a positive market price implies that the present value of its possible future earnings or user costs is zero. There is thus a difference between the economic and technical lifetimes of durable equipment[12].

We must still provide steady–state expressions for the prices of new equipment in terms of future returns. Since given the steady state, the age–specific user cost is constant over time, a simplified expression can be written:

$$(2.2.72.) \qquad p'^{(y)}_t = \sum_{z=1}^{w} p'^{(u)}_t \psi^{(0)^z} \beta^{(0)^{-z}} l'_z$$

$$= p'^{(u)}_t \sum_{z=1}^{w} \psi^{(0)^z} \beta^{(0)^{-z}} l'_z$$

This means that the capital value of investment in durables is zero and that no knowledge of the past is necessary to determine user cost and product

---

[12]This property appears only implicitly in price equations (2.2.61.–65.). If $p^{(k)}_{p,v} = 0$ for $1 < v < s$ this implies that both the stock of this good and its "input" are evaluated at a zero price so that they cancel out.

prices. A simplified relation between the present value of future returns and its cross–section estimator can now be derived. As in Section 2.1.2., the observed life expectancy of newly produced investment goods is:

$$\hat{e}_{0,p}^{(0)} = \frac{\sum_{z=1}^{w} \alpha^{-z} y_t' \cdot l_z'}{y_t'} = \sum_{z=1}^{w} \alpha^{-z} l_z'$$

There is an observation equation for the vector of prices $p'_t^{(y)}$ which relates the equilibrium value of user cost $p'_t^{(u)}$ to the biased estimator of the life expectancy:

(2.2.73.) $$p'_t^{(y)} = \hat{\varepsilon}_t \cdot p'_t^{(u)} \sum_{z=1}^{w} \alpha^{-z} l_z' \beta^{(0)-z}$$

From this, the vector of capital–value estimators $\hat{\varepsilon}_t'$ is found to be:

(2.2.74.) $$\hat{\varepsilon}'^{(0)} = \frac{\sum_{z=1}^{w} \psi^{(0)z} \beta^{(0)-z} l_z'}{\sum_{z=1}^{w} \alpha^{-z} \beta^{(0)-z} l'z}$$

It turns out once again that these observations are systematically biased in terms of their true values if prices and quantities grow at constant rates.

The contents of this section in fact provide all the information necessary to describe a price system with durable means of production. Two different ways of determining equilibrium prices have been presented, and prices or rentals of used machinery have been deduced from product prices rather than determining them. The underlying assumption has been that of a subsystem of capital goods forming a population whose rates of birth and death are governed by the laws of motion of the basic production system. Modern capital theory, however, is usually conducted within the framework of joint–production models. In Section 3.2. below, we shall demonstrate that both methods are equivalent, but first, the basic model of prices with joint production must be sketched.

2.2.3. Price Formation with Joint Production

2.2.3.1. Price Equations

Among the most puzzling problems in economics is that of determining the price of a commodity which is produced jointly with others in a single process. Though it is possible to tackle this problem formally and even to find unique solutions, no practical rule of valuation can be supplied, and it is not even assured that prices are positive[13].

This can be briefly demonstrated. With each product, there is associated at least one process of production, and sometimes more than one. The total value of output is:

$$(2.2.75.) \qquad p'Bz_t = p'Az_{t+1} + p'CBz_t$$

and, after insertion of x_t:

$$(2.2.76.) \qquad p'x_t = p'Az_{t+1} + p'Cx_t$$

This means that prices cannot be calculated directly from one another, but only by means of their joint processes. Seen from the input side, the total value of outputs equals total cost, summed over all industries, dot–multiplied by a vector of eigenrates of interest:

$$(2.2.77.) \qquad p'_t Bz_t = \beta'(p'_{t-1} + w'_{t-1}E)z_t$$

The same holds true for each individual process j. Sales of industry j exceed costs by a factor β_j:

$$(2.2.78.) \qquad \sum_{i=1}^{n} p_{i,t} b_{ij} z_{j,t} = \beta_{j,t} \left(\sum_{i=1}^{n} p_{i,t-1} a_{ij} + \sum_{k=1}^{l} w_{k,t-1} e_{kj} \right) z_{j,t} \qquad ,$$

so that (2.2.77.) holds as well per units of process levels:

$$(2.2.79.) \qquad p'_t B = \beta'(p'_{t-1}A + w'_{t-1}E)$$

If this is to be solved for p_t, matrix B (which, we note, is always invertible, for all goods are produced and all processes employed) must be inverted:

$$(2.2.80.) \qquad p'_t = \beta'(p'_{t-1}A + w'_{t-1}E)B^{-1}$$

---

[13] See, above all, Sraffa (1960).

This shows that it is not necessary that positive solutions exist; it does not follow from $B > 0$ that $B^{-1} > 0$ as well[14]. Negative prices as formal solutions can thus not be excluded, even though there is no economic meaning to be attached to them[15]. The problem may be avoided altogether by assuming that all goods can be produced separately, which is the starting point of the joint–production theory of capital[16].

2.2.3.2. Observation Equations

Prices at a given point in time can be related by estimating cross–section data. If the matrices of technical coefficients are known, we have:

(2.2.81.) $$p'_t B = \hat{\beta}'(p'_t A + w'_t E)$$

which, of course, is biased only if prices are not constant.

---

[14] The following example will illustrate: Let x_1 and x_2 be jointly produced in two processes, z_1 and z_2, such that:

$$\begin{pmatrix} x \\ y \end{pmatrix}_t = \begin{bmatrix} b_{11} & b_{12} \\ b_{21} & b_{22} \end{bmatrix} \begin{pmatrix} z_1 \\ z_2 \end{pmatrix}$$

Inverting B, we obtain $z = B^{-1}x$, where:

$$B^{-1} = \begin{bmatrix} \dfrac{b_{22}}{b_{11}b_{22} - b_{12}b_{21}} & \dfrac{-b_{21}}{b_{11}b_{22} - b_{12}b_{21}} \\ \dfrac{-a_{12}}{b_{11}b_{22} - b_{12}b_{21}} & \dfrac{b_{11}}{b_{11}b_{22} - b_{12}b_{21}} \end{bmatrix}$$

[15] On this and related problems, see the discussions in Morishima (1973, 1977) and Steedman (1976,1978).

[16] This assumption is the kernel of Schefold's (1979) solution to the problem of price formation with capital goods. See Section 3.2.2. below.

2.2.3.3. Uniform Rate of Profit III:
Accumulation of Capital
in von Neumann's Generalized Model

Given quasi–stationary prices, there is a uniform inflator $\psi^{(0)}$ and an interest factor $\beta^{(0)}$ such that:

(2.2.82.)
$$\psi^{(0)}p'_{t-1}B = \beta^{(0)}(p'_{t-1}A + w'_{t-1}E)$$

Similarly, prices on the expenditure side become:

(2.2.83.)
$$p'_t B = \alpha p'_t A + p'_t C B$$

Once again, it is possible to apply the rule:[17]

(2.2.84.)
$$p'_t C B \gtrless \alpha w'_{t-1} E \implies \beta \gtrless \alpha$$

Let $c_t = C B z_t$. Then:

(2.2.85.)
$$(B - \alpha A)z_t = c_t$$

Inserting x_t changes this to:

(2.2.86.)
$$(B - \alpha A)B^{-1} x_t = c_t$$

Solving for x_t, we have:

(2.2.87.)
$$x_t = B(B - \alpha A)^{-1} c_t$$

with matrix H^{-1} given by:

(2.2.88.)
$$H^{-1} \equiv B(B - \alpha A)^{-1}$$

Matrix H^{-1} is the joint–production counterpart of the (dynamic) Leontief inverse. By analogy to the Hawkins/Simon (1949) condition it may be required that H^{-1} be positive, in which case the dual price vector would also be positive. But in contrast to Leontief's matrix, it has not yet been proved that H^{-1} is positive.

---

[17] Feasible combinations of α and β in von Neumann's generalized model are examined by Morgenstern/Thompson (1967, 1976).

2.2.4. Summary Remarks on Price Equations

We have this section formed systems of price equations as duals to the system of quantity equations. Starting with the simplest case of a basic system, we reduced prices to the costs of intermediate inputs and of labor and resources. The criterion of time consistency, we saw, makes the basic price equation a system of difference equations. In contrast to the system of quantities, prices cannot be completely determined by the lagged variables which enter as costs, for there remains an interest factor which can be interpreted as the cost of using resources over a period of time and which introduces all the problems associated with explanations of interest in the tradition of Böhm von Bawerk.

We have made no attempt to solve the general price equation. This would have required elements of stationarity which reduce the degrees of freedom in the system, elements such as constant preference schemes, price adjustment functions, and the like. Without such devices, which operate so as to transform a general theory into a special one, no positive theory of prices seems to be at hand. If the discussion is confined to quasi–stationary prices, difficulties of this sort disappear and self–sustaining equilibrium solutions present themselves. But it must be stressed that the epistemological value of such solutions is limited, for they all rest on the assumption of stationarity over time. Concepts such as wage–price frontiers are therefore purely in the nature of comparative statics, offering no insight at all into the possible trajectories which connect one equilibrium to another.

In the case of equilibrium prices, we have approached a solution from two different directions, one from the input side and the other from the demand side. The first is typical of neo–Ricardian theory, in that it entails the rearrangement of the system in reduced form and the application of the theorem of Frobenius to find relative prices which depend on the distribution of income between labor and capital. The second approach, implicit in the work of von Neumann, infers relative prices by duality from the system of quantities. This is possible only if both production techniques and consumer demand are given, but if this is in fact the case, relative prices can be determined without knowledge of labor or resource costs, an approach which might well be termed a post–Austrian view of equilibrium pricing. In equilibrium, both methods amount to the same thing; if there is a solution to the first problem, there will be a corresponding solution to the second, and vice versa.

By the same token, prices can be determined when durable means of production are introduced. Capital theory ordinarily treats durables as by–products of producers' goods, but here we have made use of the subsystem approach developed in Section 2.1. This leads to two distinct price systems, one concerned with the prices of producers' goods and the other with the prices of used equipment. These interact with one another insofar as all processes which employ capital goods must return the same profit in equilibrium. This becomes important if age–specific schedules of capital goods performance are considered; the use of three–years–old machines must yield the same profits as the use of four–years–old ones. As with the system of quantities presented in Section 2.1.2, a solution to the price system can be found in the basic system of producers' goods. For this to be possible, a reduced system in which prices of capital goods all cancel out must be formed. This reduced system has a positive eigenvector (prices may also be inferred by duality from the reduced system of quantities of Section 2.1.2.). Once the prices of finished goods are known, those of used equipment are determined in the production of investors' goods, that is, in their own reproduction.

The price system is completed by the consideration of joint production. As a rule, however, no strictly positive solutions can be shown to exist without restrictive assumptions. Formally, the joint–production model is a general eigenvalue problem, while the structure of the problems in Sections 2.2.1. and 2.2.2. is that of a special eigenvalue problem. This is why we have not used this method in examining case of capital goods.

A common feature of all the variants of the price system developed here is that time elapses between the application of inputs and the production of outputs; the economy described here is what Samuelson/Solow (1953) have called a "sausage grinder". In Chapter 3, we shall offer a comparison and critique of several models of price theory based upon the criterion of time consistency. There is, of course, a class of models which do conform to this criterion, and these systems have been underlying to the arguments presented to this point. But there is nonetheless a class of models, the larger part of the so–called simultaneous–equation models, which scarcely seem to fit within our own analytic scheme. Before we consider this problem more closely, however, some generalizations of our system are in order.

2.3. Some Amplifications of the System

2.3.1. From Discrete Time to Continuous Time

The systems we have considered so far were all defined within a discrete time space characterized by equal time intervals and constrained by the assumption that there are exist no phenomena of shorter duration than that of a single time step $\Delta t = t_i - t_{i-1}$. In this section, we extend the analysis by relaxing these artificial restrictions. We begin with an obvious procedure, taking the state transition of quantities:

$$(2.3.1.) \qquad\qquad x_{t+1} = F x_t$$

and forming a difference term:

$$(2.3.2.) \qquad\qquad x_{t+1} - x_t = (F - I) x_t$$

the limit of which is:

$$(2.3.3.) \qquad\qquad \dot{x} = (\bar{F} - I) x_t$$

At the stationary point $\dot{x} = 0$, the input–output matrix can be substituted for $\bar{F}$:

$$(2.3.4.) \qquad\qquad x = \bar{F} x = A^{-1}(I - C)x = Ax + Cx$$

that is, the supply of intermediates exactly matches the demand for reproduction and consumption.

Let g be the instantaneous rate of balanced growth, that is:

$$(2.3.5.) \qquad\qquad \dot{x} = g x$$

Then, from (2.3.3.), we have:

$$(2.3.6.) \qquad\qquad \dot{x} + x = \bar{F} x$$

Substituting for $\bar{F}$ and reinverting $\bar{A}^{-1}$, we find:

$$(2.3.7.) \qquad\qquad \bar{A}(\dot{x} + x) = (I - C)x$$

that is:

$$(2.3.8.) \qquad\qquad x = \bar{A}x + \bar{A}\dot{x} + Cx$$

This result must be interpreted with caution, for while $\dot{x}$ is clearly a production rate, there is an ambiguity hidden in the interpretation of x. We have tacitly assumed that x remains unchanged when continuous time is introduced. If x is, say, July's output, then $\dot{x}$ denotes the change in monthly output between July 1 and July 2; it relates, in other words, the output for the month June 1 — July 1 to the output for the month June 2 —July 2. This problem arises because input–output theory, like macroeconomic theory, relates flows to flows, which makes it difficult to carry out economic analysis in terms of systems of differential equations[18].

We may once again construct an observation equation:

$$\hat{A}x + Cx = \bar{A}x + \bar{A}\dot{x} + Cx$$
$$\hat{A}x = \bar{A}(I + gI)x$$

in which:

(2.3.9.) $$\hat{A}x = (1 + g)\bar{A}$$

In continuous time as well as in discrete time, then, a bias is introduced when interindustry relations are estimated by cross–sections data. In our earlier analysis, we imposed the convention that all multi–stage productions be decomposable into as many elementary processes as there were required time steps. This was meant to introduce auxiliary intermediate goods such that for every point in time, t, there would be an elementary process φ_t with products x_t. If we now extend analysis under this convention to permit time to be measured continuously, we obtain a continuum of intermediate goods in one–to–one correspondence with the continuum of time[19]. This, however, leads to the introduction of systems of infinite dimension and, with them, to considerable problems of economic interpretation.

We have already alluded to this question. If a commodity is produced in a two–stage process which is not decomposed, the material flow within that industry will not appear in the Lexis diagram, in which kinked arrows are obtained:

---

[18]On related problems in macroeconomics, see Fowley (1975).
[19]I am indebted for this point to Professor B. Schefold, University of Frankfurt, Germany (W).

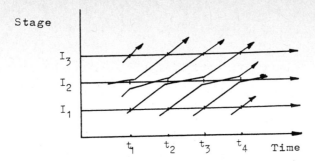

Fig. 26: Kinked Lexis Arrows With Two–Stage Production in Industry I_2

This scheme reproduces Figure 4. Because production within industry I_2 is carried out in two stages, there is a two–period delay between the application of inputs to I_2 and the final production of the industry's output. This structure may now be generalized. Let the vector x_t be an array of true industrial outputs, that is, empirically observable goods. Then these outputs themselves enter into production processes whose outputs are finished only after the passage of some period of time:

$$(2.3.10.) \qquad x_t - Cx_t = P_1 x_{t+1} + P_2 x_{t+2} + \ldots$$

$$= \sum_{i=1}^{\infty} P_i x_{t+i}$$

where the P_i are the true i–period lagged technical input–output matrices. Similarly, outputs at time t can be understood as the result of an infinite series of dated inputs, either additively:

$$(2.3.11a.) \qquad x_t = \sum_{i=1}^{\infty} (Q_i x_{t-i} + R_i r_{t-i})$$

or with fixed coefficients:

$$(2.3.11b.) \qquad x_t = \min_{0 < i,j < \infty} (Q_i x_{t-i}; R_j r_{t-i})$$

Now consider the special case of balanced growth by factor α. Equation (2.3.11b.) now becomes:

$$(2.3.12.) \qquad x_t = \min_{0 < i,j < \infty} (Q_i \alpha^{-i} x_t; R_j \alpha^{-j} r_t)$$

Moreover, since:

$$x_t = Q_1 x_{t-1}$$
$$x_{t-1} = Q_1 x_{t-2}$$
$$\vdots$$

we find:

$$x_t = Q_1^2 x_{t-2} = Q_1^3 x_{t-3} \ldots = Q_1^n x_{t-n}$$

All multi–period matrices can therefore be expressed in terms of matrix Q_1:

(2.3.13.) $$Q_i = Q_1^i \quad , \quad \text{all} \quad i$$

This will, of course, hold true only for time–invariant matrices. The steady-state system can now be written as:

(2.3.14.) $$x_{t+1} = \min_{0 \le i,j < \infty} (Q_1^{i+1} \alpha^{-i} x_t; R_1^{i+1} \alpha^{-i} x_t)$$

Here, the time indices have been changed, so matrices F and G of the state-transition function can be given by:

(2.3.15.) $$F = \min_{0 \le i,j < \infty} Q_1^{i+1} \alpha^{-i} \quad ; \quad G = \min_{0 \le i,j < \infty} R_1^{i+1} \alpha^{-i}$$

This makes clear that it is not necessary to define auxiliary goods in order to find the state–space form of the system; it is, moreover, possible to provide state–space forms for non–steady–state sequences of system states, (see Luenberger (1979), Chapter 4). Of course, matrices F and G can no longer be interpreted as technical coefficient matrices, but the state vector x is now free of dummy variables.

We come now to the transition to continuous time. If both system states and input sequences are continuous functions of time, then there will always be a functional of the form $x_{t+1} = f(Fx_t, Gr_t)$, regardless of the time scale. In continuous time, the state–transition function φ collapses into a functional $\bar{\varphi}$.

As before, let A be the input–output matrix for a given time step Δt, and $\hat{A}$ be its cross–section estimation. For arbitrary time intervals δt, the input–output matrix is then $\tilde{A}(\delta t)$. $\tilde{A}$ can be represented as a function of $\hat{A}$ which is strictly monotonously decreasing in δt. We know that $\hat{A} > A$ with $\alpha > 1$, so for $0 < dt < \Delta t$ there will be a matrix $\bar{A} = \tilde{A}(dt)$ with $A < \bar{A} < \hat{A}$. The same holds true, with signs reversed, when $\alpha < 1$. We have implicitly employed this result above. In discrete time, the input–output form of the system is given by:

(2.3.16.)
$$x_t = \alpha A x_t + C x_t$$

with the observation:

(2.3.17.)
$$x_t = \hat{A} x_t + C x_t$$
$$\hat{A} = \alpha A \qquad > A \quad , \quad \alpha > 1$$

In continuous time, this becomes:

(2.3.18.)
$$x_t = (1 + g)\bar{A} x_t + C x_t$$

Now consider now g in relation to α. Given exponential growth of production, output at time t is:

(2.3.19.)
$$x_t = x_0 e^{gt}$$

while at time $t + 1$:

(2.3.20.)
$$x_{t+1} = \alpha x_t = x_0 e^{g(t+1)}$$

This yields:
$$e^{g(t+1)} = \alpha e^{gt}$$

that is:

(2.3.21.)
$$g \cdot (t + 1) = \ln \alpha + g \cdot t$$

This provides a solution for g:

(2.3.22)
$$g = \ln \alpha < \alpha$$

which is a formal result familiar from the calculation of compound interest.

The question remains whether $(1 + g)$ is greater or smaller than α. For $\alpha = 1$ it follows that:

(2.3.23.)
$$1 + g = 1 + \ln \alpha = 1 \quad , \quad \alpha = 1$$

$1 + \ln \alpha$ is a function of α :

(2.3.24.)
$$1 + \ln \alpha = f(\alpha)$$

From:

(2.3.25.) $$f'(\alpha) = \frac{d\ln\alpha}{d\alpha} = \frac{1}{\alpha}$$

there follows for $\alpha > 1$:

(2.3.26.) $$f'(\alpha) < \alpha \qquad \alpha > 1$$

which ensures that:

(2.3.27.) $$1 + g < \alpha \qquad \alpha > 1$$

The same is true with signs reversed if $\alpha < 1$. From this, we may rely upon:

(2.3.28.) $$\hat{A} = (1+g)\bar{A} = \alpha A$$

to conclude that:

(2.3.29.) $$\bar{A} = \frac{\alpha}{(1+g)}A \quad \begin{matrix} > A \\ < A \end{matrix} \quad \text{for} \quad \begin{matrix} \alpha > 1 \\ \alpha < 1 \end{matrix}$$

as was supposed above. Equation (2.3.28.) shows that in continuous time as well there remains a difference between the dynamic and the simultaneous model, a point about which the literature has displayed some ambiguity[20]; $\hat{A}$ is still a biased estimator of $\bar{A}$.

2.3.2. A Linear Stock–Flow System

The transition to continuous time makes apparent a shortcoming of the discrete–time system employed to this point: that system formed only flow–flow equilibria in the stream of intermediates, without taking stocks other than those of durable capital goods into account. Such a model neglects inventories entirely, and it is always implicitly assumed that all quantities produced neatly meld into one another. An economy as perfectly constructed as this is simply impossible; no market or planning process is able to remove the element of uncertainty from the flow of materials entirely. Buffer stocks ("Ausgleichsvorräte", as Leontief (1928) puts it) must therefore be incorporated in the analysis. Let q_i be the inventory of commodity i, a quantity

---

[20] See, for example, Malinvaud (1953), Wan (1971), Hicks (1973).

which is increased by production x_i and diminished by demand for further use of i in production or consumption. In discrete time, we have:

(2.3.30.)
$$q_{i,t} - q_{i,t-1} = x_{i,t} - \sum_{j=1}^{n} a_{ij} x_{j,t+1} - \gamma_i x_{i,t}$$

or, in matrix notation:

(2.3.31.)
$$q_t - q_{t-1} = x_t - A x_{t+1} - C x_t$$

In continuous time, this becomes:

(2.3.32.)
$$\dot{q} = x - \bar{A} - \bar{A}\dot{x} - Cx$$

Balanced growth presupposes that stocks and flows both grow at the same rate:

(2.3.33.)
$$\dot{q} = gq$$
$$\dot{x} = gx$$

Substituting, we have:

(2.3.34.)
$$gq = (I - (1+g)\bar{A} - C)x$$

that is, a stock/flow equilibrium which is independent of time.

   This solution is not yet satisfactory, for (2.3.32.) is not a differential equation in q. Yet there does not seem to be a causal nexus between production rates and commodity stocks, and we are at best able to deduce such interrelationships from behavioral assumptions. But to do so would remove us from the solid ground of general theory to the uncertain waters of business–cycle theory.

2.3.3.   The Problem of Control I:
Leaving the Steady State

   Throughout this chapter, we have followed the traditional analytic course of fixing attention on the existence of equilibrium solutions, where equilibrium is taken to mean either stationary states or exponential change at constant rates. Contemporary system theory, however, is concerned with a rather different set of questions, among them the range of solutions which can be reached from a given initial value and the ways in which system states can be inferred from the observation of external outputs. We first consider the

problem of reachability or control, which implies that the state of the system at any given time must be under complete control of a past series of external inputs. In the case of the additive discrete–time system of quantities:
(2.3.35.)

$$x_{t+1} = Fx_t + \mathcal{D}r_t \qquad \text{where} \qquad F = [f_{ij}]_{n\times n}$$
$$c_t = Cx_t \qquad\qquad\qquad \mathcal{D} = [d_{ik}]_{n\times m}$$

the state of the system at time $t + 1$ is only incompletely controllable by the external inputs of time t, since it recursively depends on the past system state x_t as well. Substituting for x_t, we find:

$$x_{t+1} = F^2 x_{t-1} + F\mathcal{D}r_{t-1} + \mathcal{D}r_t$$

Apparently, this procedure may be repeated, and thus an infinite multiplier chain is obtained:

(2.3.36.) $$x_{t+1} = \mathcal{D}r_t + F\mathcal{D}r_{t-1} + F^2\mathcal{D}r_{t-2} + \dots$$

Matrices $\mathcal{D}, F\mathcal{D}, F^2\mathcal{D}\dots$ may be expressed as a single matrix, and complete controllability requires that matrix $\mathcal{M}$ defined as:

(2.3.37.) $$\mathcal{M} = \left[\mathcal{D}, F\mathcal{D}, F^2\mathcal{D}, \cdots, F^{n-1}\mathcal{D}\right]_{n\times nm}$$

must be of full rank n[21]. F is plainly of rank n, i.e. none of its rows and columns is zero or becomes zero after permutation[22], but the restrictions on $\mathcal{D}$ are of greater interest. It is clear that nothing can be said about the rows of $\mathcal{D}$, for there may be products which require no external inputs at all in their final production step[23]. But it is obvious that all the columns of $\mathcal{D}$ must be positive: If column k were null, no input of resource k would be needed and k could be removed from the system. In a correctly specified

---

[21] See, for example, Aoki (1976), Luenberger (1979).

[22] If the rank of F is lower than n, a lower–dimensional system of basic commodities can be constructed.

[23] That is, labor or external resources enter into these products only indirectly by means of intermediate inputs in which they are embodied. This case is ordinarily excluded by the assumption that labor is an indispensable input to all productions. But the following discussion shows that given a correctly specified system of production with basic commodities, this condition is superfluous.

input–output system, however, positive quantities of each external input are used somewhere in the production process. All the columns of $\mathcal{D}$ can thus be expected to contain at least one positive element.

Now let the rows of F be denoted by $a_i', i = 1, \ldots, n$ and the columns of $\mathcal{D}$ by $b_k, k = 1, \ldots, m$. All these vectors are semipositive, hence the scalar product of any two of them is strictly positive. The submatrices of $\mathcal{M}$ can then be represented as matrices whose elements are just such scalar products. For example, for $F\mathcal{D}$ we have:

$$
F\mathcal{D} = \begin{bmatrix} a_1' \\ \vdots \\ a_n' \end{bmatrix} [b_1 \ldots b_m]
$$

(2.3.38.)

$$
= \begin{bmatrix} a_1'b_1 & \cdots & a_1'b_m \\ a_2'b_1 & \cdots & a_2'b_m \\ \vdots & & \vdots \\ a_n'b_1 & \cdots & a_n'b_m \end{bmatrix}
$$

and it is now easy to see that $F\mathcal{D}$ is strictly positive. The same reasoning can be applied to matrices with higher powers of F. As long as the columns of $\mathcal{D}$ are linearly independent of one another, all matrices of type $F^x\mathcal{D}$ will be of rank n resp. m, corresponding to whether $n > m$ or $n < m$. We must therefore focus on the case in which $\mathcal{D}$ includes linearly dependent columns. Such an occurrence cannot be excluded a priori; indeed, the extreme case must be considered where each resources is used in only one process. The resource–input matrix then takes the form:

(2.3.39.)

$$
\mathcal{D} = \begin{bmatrix} 0 & \cdots & 0 \\ \vdots & & \vdots \\ d_{j1} & d_{jk} & d_{jm} \\ \vdots & & \vdots \\ 0 & \cdots & 0 \end{bmatrix}_{n \times m}
$$

that is, the column vectors of $\mathcal{D}$ are linearly dependent. Again, let $b_k, k = 1, \ldots, m$ be the k-th column vector of $\mathcal{D}$. Where (2.3.39.) holds, there are m scalars λ_k such that:

(2.3.40.)
$$
\mathcal{D} = [b_1, \ \lambda_2 b_1, \ldots, \ \lambda_m b_1] \quad , \qquad \lambda_1 = 1
$$

Now multiply this by an n-dimensional square matrix A, whose row vectors

97

are once again denoted by a_i'. The matrix product is:

$$
(2.3.41.) \qquad AD = \begin{bmatrix} a_1' b_1 & a_1' \lambda_2 b_1 & \cdots & a_1' \lambda_m b_1 \\ a_2' b_1 & a_2' \lambda_2 b_1 & \cdots & a_2' \lambda_m b_1 \\ \vdots & \vdots & & \vdots \\ a_n' b_1 & a_n' \lambda_2 b_1 & \cdots & a_n' \lambda_m b_1 \end{bmatrix}_{n \times m}
$$

All the columns of this matrix are linearly dependent, so the rank of AD can be no greater than 1. Controllability now requires that the rank of matrix $M = [D, FD, F^2 D, \ldots, F^{n-1} D]$ be n. Equation (2.3.39.) reveals the rank of D to be 1, and by (2.3.41) the rank of all other matrices is unity as well. Since F, F^2 and so on are linearly independent of one another, M consists of n linearly independent matrices of rank 1 and is itself of rank n.

There remains the related problem of observability. As before, let C be the output matrix of the quantity system. The system is said to be completely observable if matrix S, defined as:

$$
(2.3.42.) \qquad S \equiv \begin{bmatrix} C \\ CF \\ CF^2 \\ \vdots \\ CF^{n-1} \end{bmatrix}
$$

has rank n. Recall that C relates consumption to output:

$$
c_t = C x_t
$$

Not all products need be consumer goods; where they are not, the vector of consumed quantities may be redefined so as to comprise only consumer goods. If there are n different commodities of which $p < n$ are consumer goods, c is redefined such that $\dim(c) = p$. In the same way, matrix C is redefined so as to have dimension $p \times n$. Written out in full, C now is:

$$
(2.3.43.) \qquad C = \begin{bmatrix} 0 & \cdots & 0 & \gamma_1 & & & 0 \\ 0 & \cdots & 0 & \vdots & \gamma_2 & & \vdots \\ \vdots & \cdots & \vdots & \vdots & & \ddots & \vdots \\ 0 & \cdots & 0 & 0 & & & \gamma_p \end{bmatrix}_{p \times n}
$$

Now denote the row vectors of this matrix as $c_i, i = 1, \ldots, n$. These vectors are linearly independent, for their last p elements span the subspace R^p. We

98

premultiply a square matrix A of rank n by matrix C to obtain a matrix of rank p (for $p < n$):

$$(2.3.44.) \qquad CA = \begin{bmatrix} c_1' a_1 & c_1' a_2 & \cdots & c_1' a_n \\ c_2' a_1 & c_2' a_2 & \cdots & c_2' a_n' \\ \vdots & & & \vdots \\ c_p' a_1 & c_p' a_2 & \cdots & c_p' a_n \end{bmatrix}$$

where a_i denotes the i–th column vector of matrix A. Clearly, CA has rank p, for neither vectors c' nor vectors a are linearly dependent upon one another. Now substitute matrices F, F^2, etc. for A. Since all of these matrices are linearly independent, matrix S must have rank n and the system is completely observable. Kalman (1980, 1982) has suspected that economic systems will usually prove to be uncontrollable and unobservable. But we have seen that basic–commodity systems are always controllable, provided they have both positive inputs (that is, they are forced systems) and positive outputs (apart from input requirements).

Still, these results must not be pushed too far. As with most systems in economics, all the systems defined above neglect variations in inventories. This is reasonable only under steady–state conditions, in which inputs and outputs exactly match one another such that all markets are cleared. In non–steady states, the asynchrony of production and demand will usually lead to fluctuations of inventories, which in turn may exert some influence on future decisions. In technical terms, this implies that the matrices entering M or S are dependent on time. It thus makes no economic sense to apply systems designed for steady states to disequilibrium; all results so obtained will depend upon that misspecification and the control problem will be unduly simplified.

3.   Prices and Production in Economic Theory

3.0.   Introduction

In this chapter, the systems with which we have thus far been concerned will provide an analytical framework for a critical review of several economic doctrines of historical significance. The ground we have covered in Chapter 2 is by no means unexplored territory in economic theory. Most of these ideas have appeared at various points in the economic literature. But they have not yet been fully integrated into the body of modern economic thought.

Mathematical price theory has brought forth many models of very different kinds whose common aim to describe pricing and production on a general level. All of these models invoke system theory of a sort, and they may thus be understood as special cases of a larger, more general framework which encompasses and integrates them all. In the pages which follow, we illustrate several historically prominent equilibrium systems in this way, and we shall see that the principal differences between them are centered around the question of time consistency. By time consistency in this context we mean that it must be possible to represent a static model as the stationary state of a dynamic system without damaging its principal conclusions. This criterion has been introduced by Frisch (1935) and Samuelson (1947). It will turn out that some of the theories to be discussed here are inherently dynamic, while others are intrinsically static even in those versions which are explicitly characterized as dynamic.

We may in general distinguish between two classes of models in price theory. The first, by far the most common, consists of simultaneous equation systems which ignore the time dimension of production partially or completely, while the second includes systems of difference equations grounded in precisely the same time structure as the systems set forth in Chapter 2.

We shall consider each of these classes in turn, beginning in Section 3.1. with the class of simultaneous equation models. Our attention will first be drawn to the various incarnations of Leontief's input–output model of interindustry relations, and while it is true that these models may in fact be interpreted in a time–consistent way, we treat them in this section because of the light the analysis sheds on the problems of standard dynamic theory. We turn next to the Walrasian system which still forms the basis for the economic theory presented in elementary textbooks. Here, the problems of static theory appear in their clearest form, and we shall see that there is no way to render this theory time–consistent without destroying its principal conclusions. Last we discuss a simple production function with diminishing marginal products. Once again, its timeless version yields contradictual results, which shows that our argument does not depend on the assumption of fixed coefficients. Because this simple model consists of just one sector, its consistency remains unaffected when a time lag in production is introduced. But once we consider more than one sector and allow for intermediate products, the inconsistency reappears; it is then no longer possible to construct an aggregate production function which is independent of the rate of interest.

In Section 3.2., we review some important dynamic systems. von Neumann's model is sketched only briefly, for it lies at the base of most of the analysis contained in Chapter 2. A property common to the theory of von Neumann and of Sraffa is their inclusion of durable means of production as joint products, and we examine the relationship between this approach and the subsystem methodology employed in Chapter 2. Armed with these conceptual tools, we turn next to the theory of Karl Marx and examine accumulation with durable capital goods within the stock/flow framework of Chapter 2. As a corollary to the Marxian theory of accumulation, the properties of steady–state growth with technical progress are derived. We shall demonstrate that under steady–state conditions both the rate of "profit" and the "organic composition" of capital must remain constant. Given non-steady state conditions, the rate of profit is not necessarily equal in all sectors, hence no claims regarding its alleged secular tendencies can be made in this case.

Section 3.3. reexamines our conclusions on a more general level, viz., the state-space model of control that was sketched in Section 2.3. Value theories of all kinds are designed to reduce the problem of economic control to the control by external values such as human labor, land, or scarce resources. In Section 3.3. we hope to demonstrate that in the context of time consistency, none of these theories of external values suffices to explain prices correctly, since the rate of interest on circulating capital, which remains undetermined itself, interferes between such values and prices. In the discussion of the Marxian labor theory of value this phenomenon is known as the "Transformation Problem". We reformulate this transformation problem in a more general way and show that it applies to the theory of Walras as well. This sheds light on the problem of self–control of the economy through prices. If the system of prices was perfectly dual to the system of quantities, the array of commodity outputs could be completely controlled by the "inputs" to the system of relative prices, i.e. the prices of value–bearing inputs to production. But since the rate of interest is so difficult to determine, it turns out that price systems of such kind cannot determine the behavior of quantities. This is, the control of economic activity through exogenous values is impossible.

3.1. Simultaneous–Equations Systems

3.1.1. The Leontief System

We begin with a limiting case. Leontief, the originator of input–output theory in economics, has proposed two distinct approaches to the theory of interindustry relations. The first, set forth in two works dated 1928 and 1941, is in fact equivalent to the quantity system of Section 2.1.1, but the other, given in Leontief (1953), can be made time–consistent only by the imposition of additional restrictions are imposed which seem contrary to its author's intention.

Leontief (1941) is primarily concerned with a stationary flow of intermediates. As before, let x_t be the vector of intermediates produced in t. Then ^lA is the input–output matrix and (in the 1951 edition) c_t is the vector of consumption flows:

$$(3.1.1.) \qquad\qquad x_t = {}^lAx_t + c_t$$

which has the solution:

$$(3.1.2.) \qquad\qquad x_t = (I - {}^lA)^{-1}x_t$$

The matrix of (3.1.2.) is called the "Leontief inverse". In a short digression, Leontief (1951, p. 44) considers the problem of accumulation. By assumption, t is a period of time (in our terminology, a time step Δt). Each period describes a stationary process of production, and no change occurs within that time span. If production is to grow by, say, α from period to period, then in the present moment intermediate products must be supplied in excess of reproduction demand, so the same process will be repeated on an expanded scale in the subsequent period. Thus, the input–output coefficients for period t:

$$(3.1.3.) \qquad\qquad \hat{a}_{ij} = \frac{x_{ij,t}}{x_{j,t}}$$

would have to be divided by the growth factor in order to obtain the true technical coefficients of the economy. In our own notation:

$$(3.1.4.) \qquad\qquad \frac{\hat{a}_{ij}}{\alpha} = a_{ij}$$

This, of course, is the same logic as that of Section 2.1.1.; indeed, an early publication of Leontief (1928) even uses a Lexis diagram to portray input–output growth.

Substituting (3.1.4.) into (3.1.2.), we have:

(3.1.5.) $$x_t = (I - \alpha^l A)^{-1} x_t$$

where the matrix is the dynamic form of Leontief's inverse[1].

Moving beyond this, Leontief (1953, 1971) has sketched a dynamic model whose the formal aspects are subject to two rather different interpretations. One is to view the model as a kind of simultaneous approach (that is, as a dynamic model with embedded statics), while the alternative is to see it as a system of difference equations. The first of these interpretations is the more common[2], but it is neither necessary nor consistent[3].

Once again, let x_t be the product vector, ^lA the input–output matrix, and c_t the vector of quantities consumed. Now s_t is a n–dimensional vector of stocks of the means of production. This stock vector is connected to the flow vector by a stock–flow matrix ^lB, whose typical element b_{ij} denotes the input of stock i of the durable means of production per unit of output j[4]. The following system is thus obtained:

(3.1.6.)   (L.1.) $$x_t = {}^l A x_t + \frac{ds}{dt} + c_t$$

(3.1.7.)   (L.2.) $$s_t = {}^l B x_t$$

Differentiating (L.2.) with respect to time, we have:

(3.1.8.)   (L.3.) $$\frac{ds}{dt} = {}^l B \frac{dx}{dt} \quad ,$$

assuming balanced growth in continuous time. Substituting (L.3.) into (L.1.), we obtain Leontief's dynamic model:

(3.1.9.)   (L.4.) $$x_t = {}^l A x_t + {}^l B \frac{dx}{dt} + c_t$$

For the purposes of this section, we replace continuous time by discrete time:

(3.1.10.)   (L.4.') $$x_t = {}^l A x_t + {}^l B (x_{t+1} - x_t) + c_t$$

---

[1] For this interpretation, see Pasinetti (1977).
[2] See Dorfman/Samuelson/Solow (1958), Morishima (1964).
[3] Dorfman et al., ibid., point to this problem verbally at p. 258.
[4] Matrix ^lB is not to be confused with matrix B of von Neumann's model of joint production.

with matrices A and B appropriately redefined. We shall investigate first the conditions under which this system is equivalent to system Σ.

Equations (L.1.) through (L.4.) look like observation equations for the flow of intermediates, for inputs are there related to outputs at the same moment in time. If matrix $'A$ is to reflect the true coefficients of production, the addition to the circulation of intermediates must be included elsewhere in (L.4'.), or the system will be incapable of growth. The requisite addition is:

$$'A(x_{t+1} - x_t) \qquad ,$$

and a natural candidate for this is (L.3.), which relates stocks to flows. The simplest solution is to set:

$$(3.1.11.) \qquad\qquad s_{t+1} - s_t = {}'A(x_{t+1} - x_t)$$

This is fulfilled if:

$$(3.1.12.) \qquad\qquad 'B = {}'A$$

but this raises problems with respect to matrix $'B$, which is now no longer a stock–flow matrix of capital–goods inputs. However, the system may now be written as:

$$(3.1.13.) \qquad\qquad x_t = {}'Ax_{t+1} + c_t$$

Other solutions of $'B$ do not conform to this. Let $'B$ be such that:

$$(3.1.14.) \qquad\qquad 'B = {}'A + Z$$

where Z is the input matrix of stocks other than those required for growth. Then:

$$(3.1.15.) \qquad\qquad x_t = {}'Ax_{t+1} + Z(x_{t+1} - x_t) + c_t$$

which is not the same as (3.1.13.). An alternative approach is to take (3.1.15.) itself as the starting point. Then $'B$ is at least in part a stock–flow matrix, and there is no longer simultaneity in the flow of intermediates.

But there is an observation equation hidden in (3.1.15.) which cannot be removed, namely (L.2.). To illustrate this we reintroduce the distinction between semi–finished goods x_t and durables y_t which is rejected by Leontief himself:

$$(3.1.16.) \qquad\qquad 'x_t = x_t + y_t$$

104

where goods are so denoted as to render the spaces spanned by x and y distinct from one another:

$$(3.1.17.) \qquad {}^l x_t = \begin{pmatrix} x_1 \\ \vdots \\ x_n \\ 0 \\ \vdots \\ 0 \end{pmatrix} + \begin{pmatrix} 0 \\ \vdots \\ 0 \\ y_1 \\ \vdots \\ y_q \end{pmatrix}$$

This entails no restrictions on the technical properties of the goods; more specifically, n may be equal to q and all commodities may be appropriate for either use. Then the flow of intermediates may be given separately as:

$$(3.1.18.) \qquad x_t = A x_{t+1} + M y_{t+1} + C x_t$$

Here, M is the $n \times q$–matrix of material flow coefficients in the production of capital goods. This coefficient is unity if commodities may be used either as intermediates or as capital goods.

Conversely, stocks of capital goods may be used in maufacturing intermediates, as in Section 2.1.2.:

$$(3.1.19.) \qquad k_t = F x_{t+1} + H y_{t+1}$$

Neglecting physical obsolescence, the output of investment goods is equal to the net addition to the capital stock:

$$(3.1.20.) \qquad y_t = k_{t+1} - k_t \quad ; \qquad \delta_t \overset{!}{=} 0$$

These three equations must be forced into Leontief's dynamic model, that is, into equation (L.4'.). Toward this end, equations (3.1.18.) and (3.1.20.) are rearranged so as to fit into the stock–flow equation (L.3.'):

$$s_{t+1} - s_t = {}^l B (x_{t+1} - x_t)$$

Using matrix A and vector y_t, this becomes:

(3.1.21.)

$$\begin{pmatrix} s_{1,t+1} & - & s_{1,t} \\ \vdots & & \vdots \\ s_{n,t+1} & - & s_{n,t} \\ s_{n+1,t+1} & - & s_{n+1,t} \\ \vdots & & \vdots \\ s_{n+q,t+1} & - & s_{n+q,t} \end{pmatrix} = \begin{bmatrix} a_{11} & \cdots & a_{1n} \\ \vdots & \ddots & \vdots \\ a_{n1} & \cdots & a_{nn} \\ 1 & \cdots & 0 \\ \vdots & 1 & \vdots \\ 0 & \cdots & 1 \end{bmatrix} \begin{pmatrix} x_{1,t+1} & - & x_{1,t} \\ \vdots & & \vdots \\ x_{n,t+1} & - & x_{n,t} \\ y_{1,t+1} & - & y_{1,t} \\ \vdots & & \vdots \\ y_{q,t+1} & - & y_{q,t} \end{pmatrix}$$

105

The lower q equations of this system may again be written as (3.1.20.), that is:

$$y = k_{t+1} - k_t$$

Given balanced growth, there is again an observation equation relating inputs of capital goods to outputs of intermediates, both measured at time t:

(3.1.22.) $$k_t = \alpha(Fx_t + Gy_t) = \alpha(F\vdots G)\begin{pmatrix} x \\ \cdots \\ y \end{pmatrix}_t$$

Inserting this into (3.1.20.) we have:

(3.1.23.) $$y_t = k_{t+1} - k_t = \alpha(F\vdots G)\begin{pmatrix} x_{t+1} - x_t \\ \cdots \\ y_{t+1} - y_t \end{pmatrix}$$

This relates the difference in stocks to the difference in flows, as required by (L.3.'). Substituting into (L.3.'), we obtain:

(3.1.24.)

$$\begin{pmatrix} s_{1,t+1} & - & s_{1,t} \\ \vdots & & \vdots \\ s_{n,t+1} & - & s_{n,t} \\ s_{n+1,t+1} & - & s_{n+1,t} \\ \vdots & & \vdots \\ s_{n+q,t+1} & - & s_{n+q,t} \end{pmatrix} = \begin{bmatrix} A & \vdots & 0 \\ & \vdots & \\ \cdots & \cdots & \cdots \\ & \vdots & \\ \alpha F & \vdots & \alpha G \end{bmatrix} \begin{pmatrix} x_{1,t+1} & - & x_{1,t} \\ x_{n,t+1} & - & x_{n,t} \\ \cdots & \cdots & \cdots \\ y_{1,t+1} & - & y_{1,t} \\ y_{q,t+1} & - & y_{q,t} \end{pmatrix}$$

From here, there is a way back to Leontief's system, (L.4.'). Substituting, we see that:

(3.1.25.)

$${}^l x_t = \begin{pmatrix} x \\ y \end{pmatrix}_t = \begin{bmatrix} A & \vdots & 0 \\ \cdots & \cdots & \cdots \\ 0 & \vdots & 0 \end{bmatrix}\begin{pmatrix} x \\ y \end{pmatrix}_{t+1} + \begin{bmatrix} A & \vdots & 0 \\ \cdots & \cdots & \cdots \\ \alpha F & \vdots & \alpha G \end{bmatrix}\begin{pmatrix} x_{t+1} - x_t \\ \cdots \\ y_{t+1} - y_t \end{pmatrix}$$

$$+ \begin{bmatrix} C & \vdots & 0 \\ \cdots & \cdots & \cdots \\ 0 & \vdots & 0 \end{bmatrix}\begin{pmatrix} x \\ y \end{pmatrix}_t$$

and matrices ${}^l A$ resp. ${}^l B$ are obtained as:

(3.1.26.) $${}^l A = \begin{bmatrix} A & \vdots & 0 \\ \cdots & \cdots & \cdots \\ 0 & \vdots & 0 \end{bmatrix} , \quad {}^l B = \begin{bmatrix} A & \vdots & 0 \\ \cdots & \cdots & \cdots \\ \alpha F & \vdots & \alpha G \end{bmatrix}$$

106

Leontief's dynamic system is thus not merely a special way of describing a dynamic system with capital goods, for in its matrices both technical and observation coefficients are connected. Therefore, if a growing system is described by means of Leontief's model, the lower $(n \times q)q$ coefficients of matrix ^IB will be the greater as the rate of growth becomes larger, and conversely. In estimating a Leontief model, one does not ordinarily distinguish between investment and other kinds of commodities, and so these biases will appear unsystematically. We shall investigate the nature of this bias in somewhat more detail. One time step elapses between the completed production of a capital good and its first use in production:

(3.1.20.)
$$y_{p,t} = k_{p,t+1} - k_t \quad ; \quad \delta_{p,t} = 0$$

Once again, in each process there is one time step between the input of capital goods and the output of intermediates:

(3.1.27.)
$$k_{t+1} = (F \colon G) \binom{x}{y}_{t+2}$$

Thus, two time steps must pass between the production of new capital goods and the first unit of output produced by them:

(3.1.28.)
$$y_t \mapsto f(y_t) = (x_{t+2}; y_{t+2})$$

Leontief's model now relates the capital goods newly produced at time t to output produced at time $t + 1$:

(3.1.29.)
$$y_t \mapsto g(y_t) = (x_{t+1}; y_{t+1})$$

With balanced growth, it is always the case that:

(3.1.30.)
$$f(y_t) = \alpha g(y_t)$$

So g is an observation equation which maps a two–stage process into a one–stage process, hence the bias in estimation. From the standpoint of economic reasoning, the source of this problem is clear; standard economic theory regards inputs of capital stock as contemporaneous with outputs, and it is for this reason that (L.2.) is a simultaneous equation[5].

---

[5] There have been several attempts to incorporate gestation periods for capital goods into the analysis, see Johansen (1978) or Duchin/Szyld (1985). In these works, multi–period processes of production are assumed for the capital–goods sectors, as we have done in Chapter 2. But still the production of intermediate goods is described by static i.e. timeless equations. Hence the inconsistency of the original model with respect to the time structure of production is only partly removed.

One possible way out of this problem would be to define the time at which new investment goods are finished as the time of their first productive use. But this would require that investment be defined as:

$$(3.1.31.) \qquad y_t = k_t - k_{t-1} \quad ; \quad \delta_{t-1} \overset{!}{=} 0$$

so that investment adds to productive capacity instantaneously. Moreover, this would cause difficulties with repect to Leontief's expenditure equation, since:

$$(3.1.32.) \qquad s_{t+1} - s_t = \alpha(s_t - s_{t-1})$$

and the problem of where to include the observation equation would just be shifted from from (L.3.) to (L.4.').

A further complication arises with physical losses in the capital stock, which necessitates the inclusion of a vector δ of loss rates. δ depends as well on the rate of economic growth α; as we have seen in Section 2.1.2., the higher is α, the lower will be the mean age of capital goods. From:

$$(3.1.33.) \qquad y_t = k_{t+1} - (e - \delta)k_t$$

one finds, substituting stock inputs:

$$(3.1.35.) \qquad y_t = \alpha(F\dot{:}G) \begin{pmatrix} x_{t+1} & - & x_t \\ y_{t+1} & - & y_t \end{pmatrix} + \alpha\delta * \left[(F\dot{:}G) \begin{pmatrix} x \\ y \end{pmatrix}_t \right] \quad ,$$

which apparently exceeds the bounds of Leontief's model.

It is more convenient to view Leontief's dynamic model as a simultaneous approach. Inputs and outputs are then understood to occur at the same time moment, and economic periods are linked only by the addition to stocks. Then, again:

$$(L.4') \qquad {}^l x_t = {}^l A^l x_t + s_{t+1} - s_t + C^l x_t$$
$$(L.2.) \qquad s_t = {}^l B^l x_t$$

where ${}^l B$ is now truly a "stock–flow" matrix. Such a system is usually described as "dynamics with embedded statics"[6] There is, of course, an immediate solution which is time consistent, the stationary state $x_t = x_{t+1}$.

---

[6]This interpretation of Leontief's dynamic system has been subject to system–theoretic critique by Livesey (1971, 1974). Since matrix ${}^l B$ will ordinarily not be invertible, the system cannot be transformed to the forward–recursive state–space form; that is, it is inconsistent or misspecified from a system–theoretic view. Apparently, this is due to the ambiguous way in which time is introduced in this model. See my (1988) for details.

Then the system–theoretic approach:

$$\begin{pmatrix} x \\ y \end{pmatrix}_t = \begin{bmatrix} A & 0 \\ 0 & 0 \end{bmatrix} \begin{pmatrix} x \\ y \end{pmatrix}_{t+1} + (s_{t+1} - s_t) + \begin{bmatrix} C & 0 \\ 0 & 0 \end{bmatrix} \begin{pmatrix} x \\ y \end{pmatrix}_t$$

(3.1.36.)

$$s_t = F x_{t+1} + G y_{t+1} = (F\,\dot{:}\,G) \begin{pmatrix} x \\ y \end{pmatrix}_{t+1}$$

is equivalent to (L.4.'):

(3.1.37.)
$$^l x_t = {}^l A^l x_t + C^l x_t$$

and (L.3):

(3.1.38.)
$$s_t = (F\,\dot{:}\,G) \begin{pmatrix} x \\ y \end{pmatrix}_t$$

In the case of growth, $s_{t+1} > s_t$, this no longer holds true. Setting (L.4.') equal to (3.1.29.), we obtain:

(3.1.39.)
$$^l A = \alpha A$$

Accordingly, it follows for (L.2.) that:

(3.1.40.)
$$^l B = \alpha (F\,\dot{:}\,G)$$

This is the familiar result of Section. 2.1.: in estimating multi–stage prodcesses on the basis of cross–section data, systematic biases are introduced, with the proportionate bias equal to α.

Finally, we consider prices in Leontief's model. Leontief himself has not examined the problem of prices in the context of his own theoretical framework, though Morishima (1958), Solow (1959) or Jorgenson (1960, 1961) have done so. From the system of quantities:

(3.1.10.)
$$x_t = {}^l A x_t + {}^l B(x_{t+1} - x_t) + c_t$$

a price system is obtained as:

(3.1.41.)
$$p_t' = p_t''^l A + r p_t''^l B \, , \qquad r = \beta - 1$$

with r as the rate of profit. $p_t'^{\,l}A$ are unit input costs, while $rp_t'^{\,l}B$ are interest charges on capital goods employed. Wage costs are ignored. The second term of this price equation may be understood as the interest paid on capital.

There is an immediate solution which is time consistent. Set $^lB = {}^lA$ to yield:

$$(3.1.42.) \qquad p_t' = (1+r)p_t'^{\,l}A = \beta p_t'^{\,l}A$$

in which prices are assumed to be constant over time. In general, however, economic analysis follows the tradition of Walras to assume that there is interest to be paid only on capital stocks, and not on circulating capital. Then we have $^lB \neq {}^lA$. Insert x and s to obtain:

$$(3.1.43.) \qquad p_t'x = p_t'Ax + rp_t's$$

Interest charges on circulating capital may now be reintroduced. For this purpose, we assume once more that $^lB = {}^lA + Z$. Equation (3.1.41.) then becomes:

$$(3.1.45.) \qquad p' = p'A + (\beta - 1)p'\alpha\,[FG]$$

This makes clear that even without capital depreciation there is no time–consistent price equation, for stock inputs are being related to output at the same time, and hence there is a bias.

3.1.2. The System of Walras

With tools of critical analysis sharpened by our examination of Leontief's system, we proceed now to a discussion of Walrasian theory. The model of prices and production first published by Léon Walras in 1874 languished in obscurity until its popularization by Cassel (1918) as the First World War was drawing to and end, but then it soon became synonymous with the use of mathematical methods in economics. Those whose formal analysis incorporated simultaneous equations came to be termed the "Mathematical School", and even today it is common currency to distinguish Walrasian from non–Walrasian theory and to regard the latter as simply a special case of the former. More specifically, it is widely shared that the equilibrium described by Walras is the most general state of an economic system and that the validity of differently defined states of equilibrium is merely transitory.

In this section, I hope to demonstrate that, contrary to this conventional wisdom, Walras' theory cannot be seen as general when questions of time consistency are taken into account, irrespective of the various conceptions of stationarity or static behavior which might be associated with it.

This critique of Walras itself seems to have originated with the Austrians, beginnig with the work of Böhm–Bawerk (1889) and extending into this century in the writing of Eucken (1926) and von Hayek (1931, 1941). A modern reformulation of this criticism has been set forth by Hicks (1973). Walras was the first to offer a formal description of all the elements of an economic system of prices and production, hence the claim of generality for his theoretical scheme. But his principal results were conditioned upon his explicit neglect of the time element, and it is this omission which restricts the validity of his framework and vitiates its claim to generality. We begin our discussion with the cases of simple reproduction and price formation, and then turn to the case of durable capital goods.

3.1.2.1. Production and Prices
without Durable Capital Goods

3.1.2.1.1. Production Equations

Consider once more the formal description of system Σ, which consists of inputs u, a state vector x, outputs y and mappings G, F, and H :

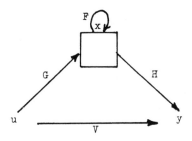

Fig. 27: Internal and External Description of System Σ

Alongside this familiar representation of the system, which is called its internal description, there exists an "external" description, the observation equation in the proper sense. The latter representation is defined by a mapping:

(3.1.46.)
$$V : u \mapsto y$$

which relates inputs of time t directly to outputs at time t without reference to the "black box". Walras' theory consists of just such an observation equation, ordinarily given in its backward–recursive form:

(3.1.47.) $$W : y \mapsto u$$

To illustrate, let u, x, and y be replaced by their economic counterparts:

(3.1.48.)
$$\begin{aligned} A &:= F & x &:= x \\ \mathcal{D} &:= G & r &:= u \\ C &:= H & c &:= y \end{aligned}$$

Walras examines a production system in which consumables c are produced from raw materials and/or labor r with the possible inclusion of intermediate products. The act of production itself is of no interest to him, so that the producer's problem is reduced to the exchange of scarce consumer goods for scarce resource inputs. The characteristic feature of Walras' model is his explicit omission of the element of time. Inputs of raw materials and outputs of consumer goods are understood to be simultaneous, implying an infinitely high velocity of production. This assumption is central to Walras' theory and has since exerted considerable influence on economic decision theory, for it enables decisions on resource inputs and commodity outputs to be taken simultaneously, without regard to potential changes in production constraints. The behavior of the economy over time is thus reduced to a sequence of mutually disconnected instantaneous equilibria wich are only secondarily combined in a dynamic calculus of resource stocks.

Formally, Walras' model connects simultaneous system inputs and system outputs:

(3.1.49.) $$r_t = W c_t$$

No reference is made to possible intermediates products, but because production itself takes no time, such intermediates may be eliminated without loss of essential information[7]. Let the flow of intermediates be characterized by the simultaneous equations:

(3.1.50) $$r_t = \hat{D} x_t$$
(3.1.51.) $$x_t = \hat{A} x_t + C x_t$$
(3.1.52.) $$c_t = C x_t$$

---

[7] Walras himself proposed such an elimination procedure. For a modern exposition see Dorfman/Samuelson/Solow (1958).

If intermediates are successfully removed from this calculation, the desired relation between resources and consumption goods can be obtained. As a first step, we have from (3.1.51.):

(3.1.53.)
$$x_t = (I - \hat{A})^{-1} c_t$$

where $(I - \hat{A})^{-1}$ is semipositive. Substituting into (3.1.50.):

(3.1.54.)
$$r_t = \hat{D}(I - \hat{A})^{-1} c_t$$

Matrix W in (3.1.49.) is then:

(3.1.55)
$$W = \hat{D}(I - \hat{A})^{-1}$$

so that intermediate products are eliminated as desired.

The problem arises as to whether Walrasian theory can legitimately be interpreted at all from the view of process analysis, for once it has been excluded, the element of time cannot be readily reintroduced[8]. Yet when the stability of Walrasian models is investigated, price adjustment functions which define prices as a function of time are generally employed[9].

The analysis which follows attempts such a reintroduction of time; we shall assume that production is goverened by the laws described in Chapter 2 above and that Walras' equations are a certain way of viewing that system of production. It is then clear that equations (3.1.50–52.) are cross–section observations of the production system and that Walras' equation (3.1.49.) is the external description of system Σ in its backward–recursive form. As is well–known from our discussions in Chapter 2, there are biases between such observations and the (causally underlying) equations of motion, which appear systematically if the production system grows or shrinks by factor α. The equations of motion then become:

(3.1.56.) $$r_t = \alpha D x_t$$
(3.1.57.) $$x_t = \alpha A x_t + C x_t$$
(3.1.58.) $$x_t = (I - \alpha A)^{-1} c_t$$
(3.1.59.) $$r_t = \alpha D (I - \alpha A)^{-1} c_t$$

which, after insertion into (3.1.49.), yields:

(3.1.60.)
$$W = \alpha D (I - \alpha A)^{-1}$$

---

[8] See Hicks (1941,1968).
[9] See, for example, Arrow/Hurwicz (1958).

113

Thus, if production grows by α, Walras' model is a systematically biased image of system Σ. In matrix W, two biases are introduced with respect to the technical coefficients, since one time step is required to transform input resources into intermediates $r_t = Dx_{t+1}$ and a second elapses during the state transition $x_t = Ax_{t+1} + Cx_t$. One might also ask the question in reverse, that is, under what conditions is there a one–to–one relation between the technical coefficients and matrix W? Such a relation, of course, exists only if $\alpha = 1$, that is, in the stationary state. For this reason, Walrasian theory cannot be reconciled with growth theory; economic growth is a temporal phenomenon, and time has no place in Walras' world.

3.1.2.1.2. Price Equations

In the same way that it views production without the roundabout processes of producing intermediate goods, Walrasian theory determines commodity prices directly from resource (scarcity) prices. Where before the element of time was neglected in production, now it is neglected in price formation. The rationale for this is that it enables commodity prices to be determined directly on the basis of input coefficients without the intervention of interest charges on circulating capital, so that only current prices are associated with one another. As is generally reckognized, *tâtonnement* is an iteration process in which no contract is performed until the equilibrium price vector is determined. Once this determination has been made, each agent retires to produce the equilibrium quantities called for, and the entire procedure is repeated in the following period[10]. There is no room even for interest on call money; this is an economy entirely free of interest calculations.

In the end, Walras produces a system of the form:

(3.1.61.) $$p'_t = p'^{(r)}_t \cdot W$$

Given some additional restrictive assumptions, there exists a strictly positive price vector to the system (see Debreu (1959)). The most prominent of these assumptions is that input resources can also be used as consumption goods and vice versa. This ensures first that vectors x and r span the same subspace of R^{n+}, second that matrix W is quadratic, and third that there

---

[10] This way of looking at the process of production is suggested by Walras himself who introduces the device of tickets (*"bons"*) which are traded in the market to determine the allocation before the act of production itself commences. See Walras (1926, par. 207.). For a modern discussion of this interpretation, see Hicks (1941).

is a preference preordering defined on the entire commodity space. Equation (3.1.61.) then degenerates to an eigenvalue problem. This means that although Nature supplies all the necessary goods, she does so in the wrong proportions, and production itself is the act of exchanging goods with Nature such as to ensure the creation of the desired proportions. This process occurs at no cost (since no time is required, cf. Roemer (1981)), and thus the prices of goods produced emerge directly from the prices of the input resources surrendered in exchange. Substitute (3.1.60.) for W to find[11]:

$$(3.1.62.) \qquad p_t' = p'_t{}^{(r)} \hat{D} (I - \hat{A})^{-1}$$

Now if Walras' approach is again regarded as a cross–section through a dynamic system, (3.1.62.) is the respective cross–section through the price system. Rearranging, we have:

$$(3.1.63.) \qquad p_t' = p_t'\hat{A} + p'_t{}^{(r)}\hat{D}$$

It is clear that (3.1.63.) is an observation equation, and it brings to mind (2.2.7.), the observation of a price system with biased technical coefficients:

$$(2.2.27.) \qquad p_t' = \hat{\hat{\beta}}{}'(p_t'\hat{A} + p'_t{}^{(r)}\hat{D})$$

These two equations are identical if $\hat{\hat{\beta}}{}' = 1$, an identity ensured by an optimization process in Walrasian theory, in which $\hat{\hat{\beta}}{}'$ is termed "excess profit".

It remains to be seen what structure is described by Walras' price system if the basic von Neumann price system is stationary and productions grow by α[12]. Walras' system then becomes:

$$(3.1.64.) \qquad p_t' = p_t'\alpha A + \alpha p'_t{}^{(r)}D = \alpha(p_t'A + p'_t{}^{(r)}D)$$

Here, α is an estimator of β, that is, Walrasian price equations describe the state of von Neumann price systems correctly if $\alpha = \beta$. This is the Golden Rule of Accumulation, already included as the optimal solution in von Neumann (1937).

---

[11] Given that the spaces spanned by p_t' and $p_t^{(r)}$ coincide as described and that some goods are basic commodities, (3.1.62.) alone suffices to determine the relative prices of a subsystem of commodities, without regard of the set of preferences. This is the kernel of Sraffa's (1960) critique of utilitarian price theory.

[12] A somewhat related discussion is Morishima (1977).

It is interesting to illustrate this result somewhat further. Walras' model has been interpreted as a cross–section through the dynamic price system. There, prices differ from unit cost by a factor β, or additively by interest payments on circulating capital:

$$(3.1.65.) \qquad p'_t = p'_t A + p'^{(r)}_t D + (\beta - 1)(p'_t A + p'^{(r)}_t D)$$

In addition, today's inputs Ax_{t+1} and Dx_{t+1} differ from those of yesterday by a factor α. The cross–section through the price system made by means of Walras' system relates current inputs to current outputs:

$$(3.1.64.) \qquad p'_t = p'_t \alpha A + p'^{(r)}_t \alpha D$$

or, additively:

$$(3.1.66.) \qquad p'_t = p'_t A + p'^{(r)}_t D + (\alpha - 1)(p'_t A + p'^{(r)}_t D)$$

Compare this to (3.1.65.). If the total value of input growth is equal to the interest charges on capital outlays, the observation is an unbiased estimator of actual price formation.

Again, the reverse question suggests itself: Under what conditions does the dynamic price system of Chapter 2 reflect Walrasian prices? In Walras' model, prices ought to emerge solely from the technical input coefficients:

$$(3.1.67.) \qquad p'_t \overset{!}{=} p'_t A + p'^{(r)}_t D$$

where A and D are here the matrices of true input coefficients. This equation holds if the third term of (3.1.65.) vanishes, that is, if:

$$(3.1.68.) \qquad r = \beta - 1 = 0$$

Therefore, in an economy whose processes take time, Walras describes an economy without interest[13].

3.1.2.1.3. Walras' Law

Multiply the Walrasian price equation:

$$(3.1.49.) \qquad p'_t = p'^{(r)}_t W$$

---

[13] This appears to resemble the Marxian Transformation Problem, and, indeed, some similarities do exist. See Section 3.3. below.

by consumption c to obtain Walras' Law:

(3.1.50.) $$p_t'c = p_t'^{(r)}Wc = p_t'^{(r)}r$$

or:

(3.1.51.) $$EX = p_t'c - p_t'^{(r)}r = 0$$

where EX is agreggate excess demand (note that (3.1.51.) also holds element by element). For system Σ Walras' Law does not hold, for with stationary prices, we have:

(3.1.70.) $$p_t'c = \hat{\beta}(p_t'^{(r)}D(I - \hat{\beta}A)^{-1})c_t$$

If interest is equal to zero, this becomes:

(3.1.71.) $$p_t'c = p_t'^{(r)}D(I - A)^{-1}c_t \qquad , \beta = 1$$

and matrix $D(I - A)^{-1}$ becomes equal to W. This result follows directly from the preceding analysis, for if production takes time, resources cannot costlessly be exchanged for finished goods and the latter exceed the former in value. Only where interest is zero this difference in value vanishes.

3.1.2.2. Prices and Production with Durable Capital Goods
3.1.2.2.1. Production Equations

In an expanded model, Walras (1877) introduces durable capital goods as a second kind of product. These are produced independently of consumption goods by means of resources and capital goods. They are used in their own reproduction and in manufacturing consumer goods. Again production takes no time. This means that there are now two production lines, one for consumer goods c and another capital goods y, and we have (see Morishima (1964))[14]:

(3.1.72.)
$$r_t = W_1c_t + W_2y_t$$
$$k_t = W_3c_t + W_4y_t$$

The average lifetime of capital goods lasts more than one time step, and a constant fraction δ of these goods fails during each unit of time. The loss rate is thus independent of the age composition of stocks. We have:

(3.1.73.) $$k_{t+1} - k_t = y_t - \delta k_t$$

---

[14] See Eatwell (1976) for a related critique of this system.

117

Once again, a multi–stage process is described by simultaneous equations. Assume that the underlying structure of production is given as:

$$\Sigma \quad : \quad
\begin{aligned}
r_t &= Dx_{t+1} &+& \ Ny_{t+1} \\
k_t &= Fx_{t+1} &+& \ Gy_{t+1} \\
x_t &= Ax_{t+1} &+& \ My_{t+1} &+& \ c_t
\end{aligned}$$

Then Walras' system defines the associated observation equations:

(3.1.74a.) $\qquad\qquad r_t = \hat{D}x_t + \hat{N}y_t$

(3.1.74b.) $\qquad\qquad k_t = \hat{F}x_t + \hat{G}y_t$

(3.1.74c.) $\qquad\qquad x_t = \hat{A}x_t + \hat{M}y_t + c_t \quad,$

albeit in reduced form. For this, the expenditure equation for x_t is reduced to:

(3.1.75.) $\qquad\qquad x_t = (I - \hat{A})^{-1}\hat{M}y_t + (I - \hat{A})^{-1}c_t$

Substituting into (a) and (b) of (3.1.74.), Walras' model which is devoid of intermediates is obtained:

(3.1.76.)
$$\begin{aligned}
r_t &= \hat{D}(I - \hat{A})^{-1}c_t &+& \ (\hat{D}(I - \hat{A})^{-1}\hat{M} + \hat{N})y_t \\
k_t &= \hat{F}(I - \hat{A})^{-1}c_t &+& \ (\hat{F}(I - \hat{A})^{-1}\hat{M} + \hat{G})y_t
\end{aligned}$$

that is, in (3.1.72.) the vertically integrated matrices W_1 through W_4 of Walras' model are solved as:

(3.1.77.)
$$\begin{aligned}
W_1 &= \hat{D}(I - \hat{A})^{-1} & W_2 &= \hat{D}(I - \hat{A})^{-1}\hat{M} + \hat{N} \\
W_3 &= \hat{F}(I - \hat{A})^{-1} & W_4 &= \hat{F}(I - \hat{A})^{-1}\hat{M} + \hat{G}
\end{aligned}$$

Given stationary production, matrices W_1 through W_4 correctly describe the integrated coefficients; given balanced growth matrices $\hat{A}$, $\hat{D}$, and so on are biased with respect to the technical coefficient matrices in the usual way, by the factor α.

3.1.2.2.2. Price Equations

Now, prices of newly produces equipment $p'^{(y)}_t$ and rentals of existing stocks $p'^{(u)}_t$ must be determined along with commodity and resource prices. In our notation, Walras' prices are:

(3.1.78a.) $\qquad\qquad p'_t = p'^{(r)}_t W_1 + p'^{(u)}_t W_3$

(3.1.78b.) $$p'^{(y)}_t = p'^{(r)}_t W_2 + p'^{(u)}_t W_4$$

Walras now completes his model with an equation which determines rentals of capital goods[15]:

(3.1.79.) $$p'^{(u)}_t - \delta p'^{(y)}_t = r p'^{(y)}_t$$

that is, interest payments on the prices of new equipment are equal to rental charges per capital good minus depreciation.

This merits some further thought. Interest arises at the input of stocks, and thus interest charges may be imputed to capital goods in just the same way as scarcity values are assigned to input resources. In a Walrasian world there are two ways to transfer wealth through time, holding stocks or holding productive capital. In equilibrium, both activities yield equal returns; and from this, Hotelling's rule follows immediately:

(3.1.80) $$\frac{p'^{(r)}_t - p'^{(r)}_{t-1}}{p'^{(r)}_t} = r$$

Note that the exclusion of the time element and its associated postulation of instantaneous production itself excludes the production of commodities from the realm of interest–bearing investment.

An obvious contradiciton arises at this point. If there is to be no circular capital and if prices are all to be determined solely by input coefficients, the production must take no time. But if production takes no time, then no time is required for the use of capital stocks either. One may thus well ask why a term representing the interest paid for using stocks could enter into (3.1.79.) at all. Interest, after all, is defined as the percentage growth of value over time, so that where no time elapses there can be no interest.

If, on the other hand, we accept the element of interest and thus an element of time in (3.1.79.), then we must also agree that inputs of flows take time, namely an elementary period of production, which in turn means that the same interest charge is due on them as is due on stock inputs. Thus, in an economy which produces commodities, there must be some interest–bearing assets other than stocks of resources or capital goods, otherwise the production of commodities would be a losing proposition compared to the

---

[15]Walras also takes insurance premiums into account. In order to illustrate these correctly, a market for stock insurance would have to be constructed, a problem which becomes rather difficult if loss rates depend on age or on the intensity of use.

alternatives of holding barren resource stocks or operating an equipment–leasing enterprise.

Once again, we take Walras' model to be a cross–section through a stationary price system with outputs growing by von Neumann's α. Matrices W_1 to W_4 are then simplified, since $\hat{A} = \alpha A$, $\hat{D} = \alpha D$ etc. Substituting these expressions into the price equation of producers' goods p'_t, (3.1.78a.), we find:

$$
\begin{aligned}
(3.1.81.) \qquad p'^{(x)}_t &= p'^{(r)}_t \alpha D(I - \alpha A)^{-1} + p'^{(u)}_t \alpha F(I - \alpha A)^{-1} \\
&= (p'^{(r)}_t \alpha D + p'^{(u)}_t \alpha F)(I - \alpha A)^{-1} \\
&\Longrightarrow \\
p'^{(x)}_t &= (p'^{(x)}_t \alpha A + p'^{(r)}_t \alpha D + p'^{(u)}_t \alpha F)
\end{aligned}
$$

Accordingly, prices of new equipment are found by substituting for W_2 and W_4 in (3.1.78b.):

$$
\begin{aligned}
(3.1.82.) \qquad p'^{(y)}_t &= p'^{(r)}_t (\alpha D(I - \alpha A)^{-1} \alpha M + \alpha N) + \\
&\quad + p'^{(u)}_t (\alpha F(I - \alpha A)^{-1} \alpha M + \alpha G) \\
&= (p'^{(r)}_t \alpha D + p'^{(u)}_t \alpha F)(I - \alpha A)^{-1} \alpha M + \\
&\quad + p'^{(r)}_t \alpha N + p'^{(u)}_t \alpha G
\end{aligned}
$$

Using (3.1.81.), this simplifies to:

$$
(3.1.83.) \qquad p'^{(y)}_t = p'^{(x)}_t \alpha M + p'^{(r)}_t \alpha N + p'^{(u)}_t \alpha G
$$

Just as in the model without durable capital goods, the cross–section is an unbiased estimator of the price system if $\alpha = \beta$. If $\alpha = \beta = 1$, the system operates with Walrasian prices, and once again, the feasible rate of interest is zero.

3.1.3. The Cobb–Douglas Production Function

Another version of the theory of productive capital is based upon the notion of a capital aggregate that is used with human labor in various pro-portions to produce goods[16]. We take as a representative example the well–known Cobb–Douglas (1928)[17]. So as to avoid aggregation problems and focus on the time structure which is of primary interest to us here, we consider

---

[16] See J.B. Clark (1888, 1899).
[17] This function has already been used by Wicksell (1913).

only the one–good version of the model, in which there are no intermediates and where input resources are free goods whose inflow is not stated explicitly. Let X be the quantity of output produced in one production step, K the stock of this good used in production, that is, capital, L the quantity of labor employed, and C consumption. All of these variables, of course, are now scalars. The model is thus:

(3.1.84.) $$x = K^a L^b \qquad a, b \in (0,1), \quad \text{ordinarily: } a + b = 1$$

(3.1.85.) $$K_{t+1} - K_t = X - C$$

(3.1.86) $$C = cX \qquad c \in (0,1)$$

The first of these equations is the Cobb–Douglas function itself, with positive but decreasing marginal returns. The total value of output can be reduced to wages and profits:

(3.1.87) $$pX = rK + wL$$

Applying elementary microtheory, we have:

(3.1.88.) $$\frac{\partial X}{\partial K} = a\frac{X}{K} = \frac{r}{p}$$
$$\frac{\partial X}{\partial L} = b\frac{X}{L} = \frac{w}{p}$$

so that real interest is equal to the marginal product of capital.

In fact, the Cobb–Douglas function presupposes a one–stage production process. But even this requires at least one time step, and so we have:

(3.1.89.) $$X_t = K_{t-1}^a L_{t-1}^b$$

Given balanced exponential growth, this becomes:

(3.1.90.) $$X_t = \left(\frac{1}{\alpha}\right)^{a+b} K_t^a + L_t^b$$

The same reasoning can be applied to the price equation. At least one time step must pass between the application of factors and the sales of finished goods, and thus interest must be charged on the total value of factor inputs:

(3.1.91.)
$$X_t = \frac{\beta}{p_t}(r_{t-1}K_{t-1} + w_{t-1}L_{t-1})$$

From this, it follows for the price equation of the Cobb–Douglas model that:

(3.1.92.)
$$X_t = \frac{r}{p}K_t + \frac{w}{p}L_t$$
$$= \frac{r}{p}\alpha K_{t-1} + \frac{w}{p}\alpha L_{t-1}$$

Now this is an observation equation for (3.1.91.). The two are equivalent if, first, all prices are stationary and, second, the Cobb–Douglas economy grows optimally: $\alpha \overset{!}{=} \beta$:

(3.1.93.)
$$\beta^*(rK_{t-1} + wL_{t-1}) = \alpha(rK_{t-1} + wL_{t-1})$$

This result is now familiar from our preceding analysis of Walrasian prices, of which Cobb–Douglas prices are themselves a special case. Some interpretation seems in order. The introduction of the element of time has changed nothing with respect to distribution in commodity terms. The product is still distributed between factors according to Euler's equation:

(3.1.94.)
$$X = \frac{\partial X}{\partial K}K + \frac{\partial X}{\partial L}L \quad a + b = 1$$

But when expressed in terms of prices, these marginal productivities become:

(3.1.95.)
$$\frac{\partial X}{\partial K} = \frac{(1+r)r}{p}$$
$$\frac{\partial X}{\partial L} = \frac{(1+r)w}{p} \quad ,$$

a result which exerts no favorable influence at all on the determination of the rate of interest.

In this simple case, however, these difficulties can be removed if we assume that interest arises solely as a consequence of investing the all–purpose commodity (i.e. capital K and advances to the workers) into a process which takes time. Given the auxiliary assumption that capital is not subject to wear and tear, we have:

(3.1.96.)
$$X_t = K_{t-1}^a + L_{t-1}^b$$

122

and, as the price equation:

$$(3.1.97.) \qquad X_t + K_{t-1} = \frac{(1+r)}{p} K_{t-1} + \frac{(1+r)w}{p} L_{t-1}$$

This leads to:

$$(3.1.98.) \qquad X_t = \frac{r}{p} K_{t-1} + \frac{(1+r)w}{p} L_{t-1}$$

This is what von Thünen (1826), pioneer of marginalist theory, seemed to have in mind[18]. In (3.1.98.), the doubled application of interest is removed, and the productivites now become:

$$(3.1.99.) \qquad \frac{\partial X}{\partial K} = r \quad , \qquad \frac{\partial X}{\partial L} = w(1+r)$$

so that the workers receive advance payments which are equal to their discounted marginal product. Clearly, no simultaneous decision on inputs and outputs is possible here, which implies that the underlying process of optimization must always be of a dynamic nature, involving constant expectations.

Once again, we may observe this model with cross–section data. Given constant exponential growth by factor α, we find:

$$(3.1.100.) \qquad \begin{aligned} X_t &= \frac{r}{p} K_t \qquad + \frac{w}{p} L_t \\ &= \frac{r}{p} \alpha K_{t-1} + \frac{w}{p} \alpha L_{t-1} \end{aligned}$$

This result is obtained if a dynamic price system is observed in the traditional way, that is, by means of an econometric model without lagged input variables.

We have seen that a period of production can be readily introduced in the Cobb–Douglas framework, albeit at the expense of general validity. But once multi–stage processes are considered, we again face the problem that interest must be paid for the use of preproducts. Of course, this implies that circulating capital is introduced. Consider a primary product X_1 which is produced from free goods by means of capital and labor:

$$(3.1.101.) \qquad X_1 = K_1^d L_1^e$$

---

[18] For a review and critical treatment see Samuelson (1983).

This product enters into the production of the finished good X_2:

(3.1.102.)
$$X_2 = K_2^a L_2^b X_1^c$$

Let us assume that each process consumes exactly one time step. Then the deflated price of X_1 is:

(3.1.103.)
$$X_1 = \frac{r}{p_1} K_1 + \frac{w}{p_1} L_1$$

while the deflated price of the finished good equals:

(3.1.104)
$$X_2 = \frac{r}{p_2} K_2 + \frac{w}{p_2} L_2 + \frac{(1+r)p_1}{p_2} X_1$$

Clearly, the last equation is conditioned upon the persistence of the steady state from $t-2$ to t. Substituting X_1 by (3.1.103.), we find:

(3.1.105.)
$$X_2 = \frac{r}{p_2} K_2 + \frac{w}{p_2} L_2 + \frac{(1+r)r}{p_2} K_1 + \frac{(1+r)w}{p_2} L_1$$

Stated in terms of marginal products, this becomes:
(3.1.106.)
$$\frac{\partial X_2}{\partial K_2} = \frac{r}{p_2} \qquad \frac{\partial X_2}{\partial L_2} = \frac{w}{p_2}$$
$$\frac{\partial X_2}{\partial K_1} = \frac{(1+r)r}{p_2} \qquad \frac{\partial X_2}{\partial L_1} = \frac{(1+r)w}{p_2}$$

Since the rate of substitution between K_2 and K_1 equals $1+r$, it is impossible to find a capital aggregate which is independent of the rate of interest. This is, a purely "technical" aggregate production function does not exist[19]

---

[19] No such complication would arise if production was atemporal. Then the production functions (3.1.101.) and (3.1.102.) could be aggregated to yield:

$$X_2 = K_2^a L_2^b X_1^c = K_2^a L_2^b K_1^{cd} L_1^{c(1-d)} = M K_2^\alpha L_2^\beta$$

where $K_1 = m_1 K_2$, $L_1 = m_2 L_2$, $M = m_1^{cd} m_2^{c(1-d)}$ and where $\alpha = a + cd$, $\beta = b + c(1-d)$. But if it were attempted to apply this production function to eq. (3.1.105.), a contradiction would be incurred, for (3.1.105.) differs from Euler's equation associated with that timeless function. Clearly, the aggregation of production functions presupposes either "timeless" or one-stage production processes.

3.1.4. Summary Remarks on Simultaneous Models

In this section, we have examined a class of models which are ordinarily called "dynamics with embedded statics". It has been seen that these models yield ambiguous results when viewed from the perspective of time consistency. Leontief's dynamic model can easily be adapted to the difference-equation form which is suggested by the results of Chapter 2. But in a truly dynamic interpretation this model loses most of its generality; since the inputs of stocks are assumed to occur simultaneously with the outputs of flows, the stock/flow structure of Leontief's model is in fact an observation equation. This assumption cannot be relaxed without affecting the principal results of the model itself.

A similar reasoning applies to the associated system of prices. There, it is conventional wisdom to calculate interest charges solely on stock inputs. So long as these stocks are interpreted as circulating producers' goods, the resulting model is equivalent to the world of circulating capital introduced in Section 2.2.1. But when durable capital goods are taken into account, an observation equation which connects stocks and flows is introduced, and thus the prices in such a system reflect the prices of a dynamic system only as distorted by a bias.

We then examine the dynamic behavior of the Walrasian system, which is the *locus classicus* of simultaneistic theory in that it explicitly excludes the element of time from the analysis. In our attempt to reintroduce time into that system, we obtain Walras' equations as observation equations in the proper sense of system theory, that is, inputs of external resources and final outputs of consumer goods are here related to one another at one and the same time. Given a dynamic production system as the underlying structure, these interrelations appear as systematically biased estimations of the dynamic system if balanced exponential growth is assumed, while, of course, the Walrasian production equations entail no bias in the stationary state. It is simply for this reason why the Walrasian system with variable coefficients cannot be employed to properly explain relative prices by means of marginal products. Since given balanced growth, Walras' "coefficients of fabrication" are of no technical nature, their derivatives have no causal meaning as well. In the stationary state, there is at least a loose connection, for the Walrasian coefficients may then be interpreted as vertically integrated input coefficients.

When prices come into consideration, the situation is even worse. Walras' familiar procedure is to reduce the prices of consumer goods to the prices of resources which are weighted by their respective coefficients of fabrication. But this is only viable if no time elapses during the process of production or no interest is calculated on the use of circulating capital over time, just as in a pure labor–value economy. Once we reintroduce time and allow for the calculation of interest, there is an element of interest which intervenes between the prices of inputs and outputs, and the Walrasian explanation of prices fails. The Walrasian system of prices can be reinterpreted as a system of external observation equations, and we have seen that it describes the price formation of the underlying dynamic system correctly if the latter obeys to the Golden Rule.

This logic applies similarly if capital goods are introduced. In the quantity system, the stock–input structure assumed in Walras' system describes observation equations, and once again, the associated coefficients can only be interpreted as vertically integrated technical coefficients if a stationary state is assumed, while in the case of balanced growth, a systematic bias is introduced.

The Walrasian price system with capital goods entails a peculiarity. Walras attributes interest payments solely to the use of durable capital goods, and he determines capital–rentals by interest charges, amortization allowances and insurance premiums. Since the calculation of interest presupposes time, this implies that there must be a period of production. But Walras does not assign interest charges to the non–durable inputs of his system, which in turn implies that there is no period of production. This contradiction is the starting point of most theories of productive capital, for in such systems, interest arises only where capital goods are used. Once again, Walras' prices are only consistent if no interest is charged at all; the observation equations described by this theory reflect prices correctly if the underlying system grows by $\alpha = \beta$.

We then examined another version of marginal–productivity theory, the Cobb–Douglas production function. In this system as well, the simultaneity of inputs and outputs is assumed, and thus it is not clear why interest on capital goods arises at all. Given the assumption that the underlying structure is dynamical, we derive some equilibrium price conditions and show that the traditional adding–up equation for the distribution of factor incomes is an observation equation. Once again, this equation describes the behavior of prices correctly in the state of optimal growth.

Production functions with a production lag have also been proposed, and it is possible to find time–consistent results here. But the seeming insensitivity of the Cobb–Douglas model to the introduction of production lags must not be pushed too far, for it is conditioned upon the existence of only one sector of production. As a counter–example, we introduce an intermediate commodity which enters as a third factor into the process of producing the finished good. Our attempt to first reduce the value of this intermediate good to its embodied factor prices and then construct an aggregate production function

126

in capital and labor fails. This is due to the fact that capital of today and capital of yesterday are different goods which cannot be aggregated without knowledge of the rate of interest. In somewhat different shape, this is a well–known result of the so–called Cambridge Controversy. We shall provide a more general expression for this problem of simultaneistic price theory in Section 3.3. below, but first, we turn to our examination of some systems of difference equations in the theory of prices.

3.2.   Difference Equation Systems

There is a number of models in economic production theory that describe dynamic structures in difference equations. This is most clearly the case with von Neumann's approach the generalization of which is the basis of Ch. 2. The stationary state of this system is to be found in Sraffa (1960) which extends the case to a general theory of value. The same dynamic element underlies the reproduction scheme of Marx.

3.2.1.   The von Neumann Model

von Neumann (1937) constructs a scheme of pricing and production in a context of balanced growth and constant prices. All products are made from other products, and no product enters into consumption. At any given time, i processes are employed alongside one another, and the process intensity at which process i is run is z_i. It may be the case that more than one kind of product emerges per process, so that there is an output matrix which relates the quantities produced to the intensity levels of production. Then, as in Sections 2.1.3. and 2.2.3. above:

(3.2.1.) $$Bz_t = \alpha A z_t$$

and, in terms of prices:

(3.2.2.) $$p'B = \beta p' A$$

Now multiply (3.2.1.) from the left by p' and (3.2.2.) by from the right by z_t to obtain:

(3.2.3.) $$p'Bz_t = \alpha p' A z_t = \beta p' A z_t$$

from which:

(3.2.4.) $$\beta = \alpha$$

127

von Neumann arrives at this result from a consideration of the optimal choice from among m processes for the production of n commodities; equations (3.2.1.–3.) may be understood as properties of the optimum state of the system. But it is apparent that 3.2.4. holds for any structure of production which fulfills (3.2.1.) and (3.2.2.) as strict equations[20]. All output x_t emerges from the processes which terminate at time t:

$$(3.2.5a.) \qquad\qquad x_t = Bz_t$$

and is channeled into the processes which occur during the time step immediately following its own production:

$$(3.2.5b.) \qquad\qquad x_t = Az_{t+1} \qquad ,$$

and all process intensities increase by the factor α:

$$(3.2.6.) \qquad\qquad z_{t+1} = \alpha z_t \qquad ,$$

though these particular equations do not appear explicitly in von Neumann's own 1937 analysis.

There exists a broad literature on the optimal control of von Neumann systems, which is founded on the turnpike theorem of Dorfman/Samuelson/ Solow (1958). In the light of these writings it is interesting to note that von Neumann's system is both uncontrollable and unobservable in the system– theoretic sense. For consider the state–space form of this system; it consists of just one homogenous system of difference equations:

$$(3.2.7.) \qquad\qquad x_{t+1} = A^{-1}Bx_t$$

In the terms of system theory, (3.2.7.) is a free system, that is, there are neither inputs r nor outputs c under consideration. Control in the sense of system theory is conditioned upon the existence of external instruments r, while observability presupposes the existence of outputs c. Trivially, if neither of these exist then both the controllability matrix M and the observability matrix S are zero.

---

[20] von Neumann's system can be generalized in either of two directions, first by admitting consumption $Cx_t = CBz_t$, and second by attributing prices to external inputs. On the former, see Kemeny/Morgenstern/Thompson (1956), Morgenstern/Thompson(1967, 1976), on the latter, Morishima (1964, 1973, 1978).

The system of von Neumann is also the underlying structure of those equilibrium systems which are based on dynamic activity analysis. For let the input and output vectors be rewritten as a and b, respectively. Then (3.2.2.) changes to:

$$(3.2.8.) \qquad\qquad p'_{t+1} b_{t+1} = \beta p'_t a_t$$

General equilibrium theory is ordinarily concerned with discounted prices such that $\tilde{p}_{i,t}$ is the present value of commodity i to be delivered at time t as evaluated at time 0. (3.2.8.) is then equivalent to the zero-profit condition:

$$(3.2.9.) \qquad\qquad \tilde{p}'_{t+1} b_{t+1} = \tilde{p}'_t a_t$$

(for a proof see Hausman (1981)). This way of denoting equilibrium makes it possible to express the whole system in the manner of static Walrasian theory without running into its logical difficulties. The problem of optimal intertemporal allocation is thus formally reduced to the static problem of optimum choice as known from standard Walrasian theory. See Debreu (1959). Note that equilibrium in the sense of a constant rate of interest does not necessarily entail a steady state in the quantity system as long as a variety of production techniques is assumed. Hence it has often been claimed that this system is the most general existing approach to price theory. But even for such a steady state to persist, it must be assumed that after the beginning of the planning period no unpredicted change in the state of the world occurs, just as is the case with turnpike theory in the von Neumann model. Hence it does not provide more information regarding actual price formation than does any dynamic production system upon which a zero-profit condition is imposed.

3.2.2. The System of Sraffa

3.2.2.1. Price Equations

Picro Sraffa's system is a limiting case of dynamic theory. He refers to the "long period" characteristic of classical analysis and derives prices which are consistent in the long run and lead to a uniform rate of profit. Sraffa's model pretends to include no restrictions regarding production coefficients, consisting solely of a system of value equations:

$$(3.2.10.) \qquad\qquad p'B = \beta p'A + wu'$$

where w is the wage rate of unskilled labor and u' is its input vector. Employing a cost–of–production approach, all forms of higher–quality labor are reduced to common labor. All production steps are of equal duration, commodity inputs are due at the beginning of this period and command interest, and wages are paid at the end of the period. In this way, Sraffa postulates a stationary price system. He argues in terms of given process intensities and a given technique, with no assumption with respect to technical choice and on the volume of outputs[21]. Clearly, this may be interpreted as a difference–equation system at its stationary point:

$$(3.2.11.) \qquad p_t' B = \beta p_{t-1}' A + w_t u \quad , \quad p_t' = p_{t-1}'$$

Like Walras and Arrow/Debreu, Sraffa does not examine the way in which prices are actually formed. Where Walras assumes the stylized process of *tâtonnement* and where Arrow/Debreu employ the idea of contingent markets, Sraffa postulates a long period which is understood as the gravitational center of market prices. His approach is consistent with dynamic reasoning if his model is interpreted as a stationary price system[22]. We have already seen that Walrasian prices are correctly reflected in the stationary system of Chapter 2 only where the rate of interest is zero. But this is not the case here, and as Roncaglia (1978) shows, Sraffa's system can even be extended to include the payment of wages in advance. In this case, there is $\tilde{w}$ such that:

$$(3.2.12.) \qquad p'B = \beta(p'A + \tilde{w}u') \quad \tilde{w} = \beta^{-1}w$$

which corresponds to the results of Section 2.2.1. above.

It is interesting to investigate the relationship between this model and that of Walras. Walras' model has been shown to be equivalent to:

$$(3.1.62.) \qquad p' = p'^{(r)} \hat{D}(I - \hat{A})^{-1}$$

Adapting the notation, we shall assume that $p'^{(r)}D$ represents Sraffa's uniform labor, and we shall for the moment assume as well that there is no joint production. With wages paid in advance, Sraffa's system becomes:

$$(3.2.13.) \qquad p' = \beta(p'A + p'^{(r)}D)$$

---

[21] This is why no assumptions regarding returns to scale are necessary.

[22] Stationary prices must be mutually consistent or they will not continue to be stationary. But the question remains as to what a "long period" of price formation is when constant techniques are not assumed. Long periods in which techniques do change are not conductive to the gravitation of prices toward equilibrium. It seems reasonable to look at Sraffa's system as a way to determine the set of prices which is consistent with a given production technique.

or, after rearranging terms:

$$(3.2.14.) \qquad p' = p'^{(r)} D(I - \beta A)^{-1}$$

Now suppose that matrices $\hat{A}$ and $\hat{D}$ in (3.1.62.) reflect technical coefficients correctly, which they in fact do in the stationary state. Then Sraffa's prices collapse into Walras' prices if $\beta = 1$, that is, when the rate of interest is zero. Thus, at least with respect to time consistency, Sraffa's prices do not emerge as a special cases of Walras'prices, as, for example, Burmeister (1980) would argue; instead, just the reverse seems to be the case.

3.2.2.2. Durable Capital Goods

Following Schefold (1979), we now incorporate durable capital goods into the analysis. We make no distinction between producers' goods x and capital goods y; together, they form the vector x^+. Let us assume that there is but one kind of commodities i produced in each process process i, so that used machinery is the only joint product (no superimposed joint production, as Schefold puts it). We assume further that all industries may be decomposed into w subindustries z, in each of which only machinery and equipment of age z are employed. There are thus w different z–techniques, each identified by the age of its equipment[23]. Then the output of commodity i in industry i is:

$$(3.2.15.) \qquad x^+_{i,z} = b_{ii,z}\zeta_{i,z_t}$$

Here ζ has been substituted for process intensities z in order to avoid confusion with the age cohorts z. Similarly, the input of commodiy j in z–industry i is:

$$(3.2.16.) \qquad x^+_{ji,z,t} = a_{ji,z}\zeta_{j,z,t+1}$$

The input of machinery of type p and age z in producing commodity i is:

$$(3.2.17.) \qquad k_{qi,z,t} = s_{qi,z}\zeta_{i,z,t+1}$$

Capital goods emerge from production aged by one time step:

$$(3.2.18.) \qquad k_{qi,z+1,t+1} = \overline{s}_{qi,z,t+1}\zeta_{i,z,t+1}$$

---

[23]Note that we have employed an identical assumption in Section 2.1.2. above.

There are thus input coefficients a_{ji} and output coefficients b_{ii} for each commodity and, similarly, there are input coefficients s_{qi} and output coefficients $\bar{s}_{qi}$ for each type of machinery. Taken together, these form input and output matrices A_z, B_z, S_z, and $\bar{S}_z$, respectively. Let the prices of commodities be $p'^{(z^+)}$ and the prices of z–aged equipment be $p'^{(k)}_z$. Measured per unit of process intensities ζ_z, there is in each age cohort of industries z a system of price equations like:

$$(3.2.19.) \qquad \beta(p'^{(z^+)}A_z + p'^{(k)}_z S_z + wu'_z) = p'^{(z^+)}B_z + p'^{(k)}_{z+1}\bar{S}_{z+1}$$

Now in order to determine prices of equipment of age z, we must have a system which determines the prices of finished goods $p'^{(z)}$ independently of these equipment prices. We can derive such a system if, for each industry i, the price equation of age cohort i is discounted by β^{-z} and all the equations are added together. Consider the following example. We assume a two–stage process of production in which a machine is used up. The new equipment must be purchased at time t, and together with the demand for intermediates this involves prime costs which amount to $p'^{(z^+)}A_0$ per unit of the process level. The equipment is now employed as a tool in the production process to follow. At time $t + 1$, the outputs are sold, and together with the second–hand price of the machine the revenues are $p'^{(z^+)}B_1 + p'^{(k)}S_1$. Our machine has now survived to the mid of its lifetime and is good for still another use in production. For this second process, intermediates must be purchased at time $t+1$, and together with the second–hand price of the machine, costs incurred are $p'^{(z^+)}A_1 + p'^{(k)}S_1$. This second process yields revenues $p'^{(z)}B_2$ from the sale of intermediate goods at time $t + 2$, while the machine is worn out now and its value reduced to zero. If now all costs and revenues incurred during the lifetime of the machine are summed up, we obtain a system of prices which is independent of the prices of used machinery. Unit costs have been $p'^{(z)}(A_0 + \beta^{-1}A_1)$ in total while unit revenues have been: $p'^{(z)}(\beta^{-1}B_1 + \beta^{-2}B_2)$. From the standpoint of the Lexis diagram, this aggregation is a cohort analysis of capital goods, as in Figure 28:

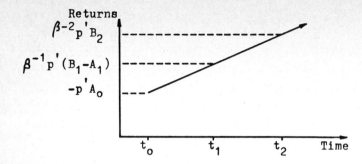

Fig.28: Cohort Analysis of Pricing With Durable Capital Goods

On the vertical axis of Figure 28, we have represented the present value of net revenues, with time denoted on the horizontal axis. After two periods, $(t+2)-(t+1), (t+1)-t$ machines have worn out and been reduced in value to zero; their second–hand prices have cancelled out. The example may be extended to processes of arbitrary duration, though here, contrary to the assertions of both Sraffa himself and his followers, the assumption of stationary techniques, constant returns to scale and balanced growth (or decline) becomes truly indispensable, or time–dependent quasi–rents arise and the rate of interest is no longer uniform. If machinery is eliminated in this way, the discounted input and output matrices may be aggregated, and the integrated price system results[24]:

(3.2.20.) $$\beta p'^{(z^+)} \tilde{A} + wu' = p'^{(z^+)} \tilde{B}$$

In the two–stage case we have:

(3.2.21.) $$\beta p'^{(z^+)}(A_0 + \beta^{-1}A_1) = p'^{(z^+)}(B_1 + \beta^{-1}B_2)$$

where:

(3.2.22.) $$\tilde{A} = A_0 + \beta^{-1}A_1 \qquad \tilde{B} = B_0 + \beta^{-1}B_2$$

---

[24]It may be noted that we must, of course, assume that the proportions in which the age cohort z leaves process z, $\overline{S}\zeta_z$, are compatible with the proportions in which this cohort is employed in the process $z+1$ which follows, $S_{z+1}\zeta_{z+1}$.

It is important to note that this aggregation is not independent of the rate of interest. If matrices A and B cannot be decomposed and no two commodities are produced in a single process, the system has a solution which is strictly positive in prices (see Schefold (1979)). If some commodities are pure capital goods y, indecomposability is maintained if at least for one z there is an indecomposable matrix of capital–goods inputs S_z; in this case, all machinery is required either directly or indirectly for all producers' goods, that is, machines are basic commodities.

It remains to be seen how this approach can be transformed into the model of Chapter 2. Assume that in each age cohort z, there is only one process i, z for manufacturing goods i, that is, there are no other commodities j produced by process i. Then for the vector x_z^+ of commodities produced with equipment of age z, the output matrix B_z degenerates into a diagonal matrix:

$$(3.2.23.) \qquad x_{t,z}^+ = B_z \zeta_{t,z} \qquad \text{with} \quad B_z = \begin{bmatrix} b_{11} & & 0 \\ & \ddots & \\ 0 & & b_{nn} \end{bmatrix}$$

The concept of process intensities may thus be dispensed with altogether, for each of these can now be measured by the output of the sole product of the process. Accordingly, the input of z–old machines into z–processes (see Orosel (1977) for a related decomposition):

$$(3.2.24.) \qquad k_{t,z} = S_z \zeta_{t+1,z} \qquad ,$$

can be represented as the input per unit produced:

$$(3.2.25.) \qquad k_{t,z} = S_z B_z^{-1} x_{t+1}^{(+)}$$

Inspection of B in (3.2.23.) makes clear that B^{-1} is strictly positive, and we have:

$$(3.2.26.) \qquad F_z = S_z B_z^{-1}$$

Machines emerge from the process aged by one time step, and their proportions are possibly changed by physical losses. Defining T as the diagonal matrix of such losses, (3.2.19.) can then be written as:

$$(3.2.27.) \qquad \beta(p'^{(z)} A_z B_z^{-1} + p'^{(k)}_z F_z) + wu' B_z^{-1} = p'^{(z)} + p'^{(k)}_{z+1} T_z F_z$$

If matrix A and input vector u' are suitably redefined, we are back once again in the world of Section 2.2.2. This shows that it makes no difference whether machines are regarded as joint products or not, for with only one process per manufactured commodity, production processes can be identified with their outputs in any case. What does matter is the decomposition of the aggregate technique of production into age–specific z–techniques, for the decline in value of a piece of equipment between age z and age $z+1$ can then be derived from the properties of technique z.

In practice, this decomposition will only rarely be possible. Old trucks run with new engines (and these may themselves be modernized), and in factories, old machines are used alongside new ones; by combining equipment of different ages, a continuum of techniques which are linearly independent of the z–techniques may be realized. In this case, the method of valuation sketched here, like all other methods, is doomed to failure.

3.2.3. The Reproduction Scheme of Marx

3.2.3.1. Marx's Original Equations

In the second volume of 'Capital' (1885), Karl Marx offers price equations but no quantities, which renders the representation of his system somewhat difficult. Input–output techniques are usually invoked toward this end as in the work of Okishio (1963) and Morishima (1964, 1973), but before we too adopt this convention, we shall take a more forthright approach to Marx, the representation of his model in his own terms. In all that follows, we shall ourselves concern with prices rather than values.

As is well–known, Marx presupposes two "departments of production" I and II. The products of department I are used both for their own reproduction and as inputs to II, while the products of II are pure consumer goods, possibly with local intermediates. Value created in department I shall be denoted I_w, it is equal (in prices) to the sum of total costs incurred, that is, product inputs or constant capital I_c plus the wage bill or variable capital I_v, to which is added the surplus value I_s:

(3.2.28.)
$$I_w = I_c + I_v + I_s$$

The term:

(3.2.29.)
$$I_k = I_c + I_c$$

is the cost price of production (Marx (1894)), and, in our notation:

(3.2.30.)
$$\beta - 1 = p' = \frac{I_s}{I_k}$$

135

is the rate of profit. Accordingly, the rate of surplus value is:

(3.2.31.) $$s' = \frac{I_s}{I_v} = (\beta - 1)\frac{I_k}{I_v}$$

The same relations hold in department II:

(3.2.32.) $$II_w = II_c + II_v + II_s \quad,$$

and given stationary prices, we can expect that a uniform rate of profit will prevail in both departments:

(3.2.33.) $$\beta - 1 = \frac{I_s}{I_c + I_v} \overset{!}{=} \frac{II_s}{II_c + II_v}$$

This does not mean that the rates of surplus values are identical:

(3.2.34.) $$\frac{I_s}{I_v} \overset{>}{\underset{<}{}} \frac{II_s}{II_v}$$

Given constant prices and profit rates, these terms change only by the rate of change in physical output. In equilibrium, it must be true that:

(3.2.35.) $$I_{w,t} = I_{c,t+1} + II_{c,t+1}$$

We consider first the stationary state, that is, simple reproduction. Then, from $I_{w,t} = I_{w,t+1}$ and so on, we have:

(3.2.36.) $$I_{w,t} - I_{c,t} = I_{v,t} + I_{s,t} = II_{c,t}$$

so that the output of consumer goods exactly meets the demand for consumption out of wages and realized surpluses; equation (3.2.36.) is given by Marx himself. Substituting into II_w, we indeed find:

(3.2.37.) $$II_w = I_v + I_s + II_v + II_s$$

Now consider extended reproduction, that is, the expansion of scale by the factor α. The output of department I must now be sufficient to supply constant capital for both departments at this expanded scale, so that (3.2.35.) becomes:

(3.2.38.) $$I_{w,t} = \alpha(I_{c,t} + II_{c,t})$$

136

If accumulation is to occur, a portion of net value added $I_{(v+s)}$ in I must be withheld from consumption, in which case only a fraction $(I_{s,t})/x, \quad x > 1$ of the surplus value is consumed, and:

$$(3.2.39.) \qquad I_{v,t} + \frac{I_{s,t}}{x} = II_{c,t}$$

This condition as well appears in Marx (1885). Savings expressed as a fraction of the surplus value are then equal to investment in constant capital in both departments:

$$(3.2.40.) \qquad \frac{(x-1)I_{s,t}}{x} = (\alpha - 1)(I_c + II_c)_t$$

If this is the case, then the supply from II also finds its demand:

$$(3.2.41.) \qquad II_{w,t} = II_{(c+s+v),t}$$
$$= I_{v,t} + \frac{I_{s,t}}{x} + II_{(v+s),t}$$

so that:

$$(3.2.42.) \qquad II_{w,t} = I_{(v+s),t} + II_{(v+s),t} - (\alpha - 1)(I_c + II_c)_t$$

The sources of savings thus do not matter; at least in its formal apparatus, Marx's scheme requires no hypothesis at all regarding the distribution of savings between workers and capitalists[25].

Before articulating the equilibrium condition of extended reproduction (1885; Chapter 21, Subsection III.3), Marx wrestles with the problems of unbalanced growth, which he illustrates in a series of lengthy numerical examples. The source of the difficulty is that $\alpha_I \neq \alpha_{II}$. If, for example:

$$(3.2.43.) \qquad \frac{(x-1)I_{s,t}}{x} > (\alpha_I - 1)I_{c,t} + (\alpha_{II} - 1)II_{c,t}$$

then there is overproduction in department I. Since not all of the product of I finds its way to customers, we find for department II:

$$II_w = I_{(v+s),t} + II_{(v+s).t} - (\alpha_I - 1)I_{c,t} - (\alpha_{II} - 1)II_{c,t}$$
$$(3.2.44.) \qquad > II_w^{\text{eff.}} = I_{(v+s)} + II_{(v+s)} - \frac{(x-1)I_s}{x}$$

---

[25] This is in contrast to more traditional interpretations, see, for example, Sweezy (1952).

that is, II faces overproduction as well; the effective demand for consumer goods is insufficient. This is in fact a manifestation of the Marxist theory of general overproduction in which no widespread crisis in sales is needed to explain the general glut. Disparities between the stages of production which lead to a shortage of capital in one industry and overproduction in the other are all that is required to account for the problem, a striking, refracted echo of later monetary theories of capital shortage[26].

Consider now the alleged tendency of the rate of profit to fall. The logical possibility of such a decline has long been doubted, for with production technique given, profits become a decreasing function of wages (see Robinson (1942) and Samuelson (1957)). With technical progress, however, this will no longer be the case, and the controversy remains unsettled to this day[27].

Marx himself (1894) makes two related propositions with respect to the rate of profit. This first is a general claim that the rate of profit falls as the organic composition of capital rises, while the second suggests that in the course of capitalist development in particular, downward pressure on the rate of profit will be exerted by the increases in the organic composition of capital brought about by improvements in production technology. Consider the more general proposition first. Let the rate of growth for any given variable x be:

$$g_x = d \log x / dt$$

As before, we have:

$$s' = \frac{s}{v} \quad ; \quad c' = \frac{c}{v} \quad ; \quad p' = \frac{m}{c+v}$$

with s' the rate of surplus value, c' the organic composition of capital[28], and p' the rate of profit. Then:
(3.2.45.)

$$
\begin{array}{llll}
(a) & s' = \text{const.} & \Longrightarrow & g_s = g_v \\
(b) & g_{c'} > 0 & \Longrightarrow & g_c > g_v \\
(c) & g_c > g_v & \Longrightarrow & g_{(c+v)} > g_v = g_s \\
(d) & g_{(c+v)} > g_s & \Longrightarrow & g_{p'} = g_s - g_{(c+v)} < 0
\end{array}
$$

---

[26] See, for example, von Hayek (1931). A review of such pre–Keynesian debates which remains vaulable today is Löwe (1926).

[27] See Roemer (1981) for a review.

[28] Marx defines this term precisely only in a footnote in (1894, Chapter 13).

The first proposition thus turns out to be true, as is well known. But as the counterexamples first offered by Samuelson (1957) and Okishio (1963) make clear, the existence of technical progress places the veracity of the second in some doubt.

To illustrate, we briefly turn to the issue of neutral progress. Progress is neutral if it acts to augment labor productivity (Robinson (1938)). With prices and profits, including the wage paid to labor, constant, the organic composition of capital will rise:

$$(3.2.46.) \qquad \left(\frac{c}{v}\right)_t = \left(\frac{c}{v}\right)_0 \cdot e^{mt}$$

so that:

$$(3.2.47.) \qquad g_c - g_v = m$$

Now let wages vary by, say, μ. Then there is an organic composition:

$$(3.2.48.) \qquad \frac{\bar{c}}{\bar{v}} = \frac{c_0 e^{mt}}{v_0 e^{\mu t}}$$

and

$$(3.2.49.) \qquad g_{\bar{c}} - g_{\bar{v}} = m - \mu$$

If:

$$(3.2.50.) \qquad m = \mu$$

the organic composition of capital remains constant. For this to be the case, wages must rise as fast as the efficiency of labor inputs, a well–known result of growth theory. If prices are constant, the rate of surplus value is constant as well, and the Marxian system can be characterized as Harrod–neutral progress[29].

3.2.3.2. Input–Output Interpretation

We have thus far avoided employing the notions of input–output analysis and a quantity system, which have by now become familiar tools of Marxist theory. Marx himself repeatedly stresses the need to take account of multi-period turnover of capital and durable goods, and thus capital goods k_t are

---

[29] Again, see Schefold (1979).

made necessary. Moreover, department I produces commodities which physically enter into both their own reproduction and the output of department II. Durable capital goods and intermediates are employed in II, in which consumer goods $\tilde{x}_t = c_t$ are produced. Following Chapter 2, we may add yet another input–output model to Marxian theory:

(3.2.51a.)
$$x_t = Ax_{t+1} + My_{t+1} + Z\tilde{x}_{t+1}$$
$$k_t = Fx_{t+1} + Gy_{t+1} + H\tilde{x}_{t+1}$$
$$\tilde{x}_t = c_{t+1}$$
$$y_t = k_{t+1} - (e - \delta_t) * k_t$$
$$l'_t = l'_1 x_{t+1} + l'_2 y_{t+1} + l'_3 \tilde{x}_{t+1}$$

or in matrix notation:

(3.2.51b.)
$$\begin{pmatrix} x \\ k \\ \tilde{x} \end{pmatrix}_t = \begin{bmatrix} A & M & Z \\ F & G & H \\ 0 & 0 & 0 \end{bmatrix} \begin{pmatrix} x \\ y \\ \tilde{x} \end{pmatrix}_{t+1}$$

Given balanced growth, we have, as before:

(3.2.52.)
$$\begin{pmatrix} x \\ y \end{pmatrix}_t = \begin{bmatrix} A & M \\ \Gamma^{-1}F & \Gamma^{-1}G \end{bmatrix} \alpha \begin{pmatrix} x \\ y \end{pmatrix}_t + \alpha \begin{bmatrix} Z \\ H \end{bmatrix} \tilde{x}_t$$

which is the equilibrium level of production in department I, which can roughly be seen as the basic system. The outflows to consumption in the system of Section 2.1.2. are replaced here by outflows to department II, and with output requirements $\tilde{x}$ given, this system can be shown to have a strictly positive eigenvector $\binom{x}{y}$. In department I, there is a corresponding price system:

(3.2.53.)   (I) $(p'^{(x)} p'^{(k)}) = \beta \left((p'^{(x)} p'^{(u)}) \begin{bmatrix} A & M \\ F & G \end{bmatrix} + w(l'_1 l'_2) \right)$

Again assuming age–specific z–techniques, a self–sustained solution to this price system exists (see Section 2.2.); but prices may also be inferred by duality from (3.2.52.). With prices determined in I, we can solve for prices in the manufacture of consumer goods:

(3.2.54.)   (II) $p'^{(\tilde{x})} = \beta \left[(p'^{(x)} p'^{(u)}) \begin{bmatrix} Z \\ H \end{bmatrix} + wl'_3 \right]$

We can arrange these equations in additive form:

$$(p'^{(x)}p'^{(y)})\begin{pmatrix} x \\ y \end{pmatrix} =$$

(3.2.55a.)
$$= (p'^{(x)}p'^{(u)})\begin{bmatrix} A & M \\ F & G \end{bmatrix}\begin{pmatrix} x \\ y \end{pmatrix} + w(l_1' l_2')\begin{pmatrix} x \\ y \end{pmatrix}_t + (\beta-1)[\ ]$$

$$= \qquad I_c \qquad + \qquad I_v \qquad + \qquad I_s$$

$$\text{with: } I_s = (\beta-1)(p'^{(x)}p'^{(y)})\begin{pmatrix} x \\ y \end{pmatrix},$$

while for department II:

(3.2.55b.)
$$p'^{(\tilde{x})}\tilde{x} = (p'^{(x)}p'^{(u)})\begin{bmatrix} Z \\ H \end{bmatrix}\tilde{x}_t + wl_3' + (\beta-1)p'^{(\tilde{x})}\tilde{x}$$

$$\mathrm{II}_w = \qquad \mathrm{II}_c \qquad + \mathrm{II}_v + \qquad \mathrm{II}_s$$

The reduced system of quantities (3.2.52.) may now be regarded as a reduced or integrated system of constant capitals. Multiplying by prices, we have:
(3.2.56.)
$$(p'^{(x)}p'^{(y)})_t\begin{pmatrix} x \\ y \end{pmatrix}_t = (p'^{(x)}p'^{(y)})\begin{bmatrix} A & M \\ \Gamma^{-1}F & \Gamma^{-1}G \end{bmatrix}\alpha\begin{pmatrix} x \\ y \end{pmatrix}_t + p'^{(\tilde{z})}\alpha\begin{bmatrix} Z \\ H \end{bmatrix}\tilde{x}_t$$

which is just the condition for equilibrium growth of constant capital:

(3.2.57.) $$I_w = \alpha(I_c + \mathrm{II}_c)$$

Note that (3.2.57.) is fundamental to the Marxian system in three senses. First, it comprises the condition of equilibrium in extended reproduction; second, it determines equilibrium quantities; and third, if the device of determining equilibrium prices through the use of z–techniques is not accepted, (3.2.57.) can be used instead to help determine these prices.

3.2.3.3. Technical Progress and the Rate of Profit

Finally, we examine technical progress. Consider the case in which the efficiency of labor inputs to department I grows exponentially at rate m. Assume further that durable capital goods have been aggregated away. Then there is an integrated price system:

(3.2.58.) (I) $$(p'^{(x)}p'^{(y)})_t = \beta_t\left[(p'^{(x)}p'^{(y)})\begin{bmatrix} \widetilde{A} & M \\ F & G \end{bmatrix} + we^{-mt}(l_1' l_2')_0\right]$$

in which[30]:

$$\widetilde{[\ ]} = \begin{bmatrix} \tilde{A} & \tilde{M} \\ F_1 & G_1 \end{bmatrix}$$

If the rate of profit is to be constant and prices unchanged, differentiation with respect to time yields:

(3.2.59.)
$$\frac{d}{dt}p'^{(x)} = \frac{d}{dt}p'^{(y)} = \frac{d}{dt}\beta \overset{!}{=} 0 \implies \frac{dw}{dt}\frac{1}{w} \overset{!}{=} m$$

which is the familiar condition of Harrod–neutral progress. It is clear that the organic composition of capital remains constant, for:

(3.2.60.)
$$w(l_1' l_2') = w_0 e^{mt}(l_1' l'2)_0 e^{-mt} = \text{const.}$$

Other forms of technical progress are not neutral, nor do they allow for steady–state results. Consider, for example, the case of progress manifested in changed material–input coefficients. Then there is a matrix Ω acting on coefficients:

(3.2.61.)
$$(p'^{(x)} p'^{(y)}) = \beta \left((p'^{(x)} p'^{(y)})\Omega \begin{bmatrix} \tilde{A} & \tilde{M} \\ F_1 & G_1 \end{bmatrix} + w(l_1' l_2') \right)$$

After two periods, this becomes $\Omega^2 \widetilde{[\ ]}$ and so on. Clearly, the eigenvalue problem posed by 3.2.61.:

(3.2.62.)
$$(p'^{(x)} p'^{(y)}) \left(I - \beta_1 \Omega \begin{bmatrix} \tilde{A} & \tilde{M} \\ F_1 & G_1 \end{bmatrix} \right) = \beta_1 w(l_1' l_2')$$

is different from the eigenvalue problem of (3.2.58.):

(3.2.63.)
$$(p'^{(x)} p'^{(y)}) \left(I - \beta \begin{bmatrix} \tilde{A} & \tilde{M} \\ F_1 & G_1 \end{bmatrix} \right) = \beta w(l_1' l_2')$$

After two periods, (3.2.62.) changes to a new system, with a new eigenvector, a new eigenvalue and so forth[31]. In contrast, (3.2.60.) shows that neither side of (3.2.63.) is affected by Harrod–neutral progress. In the case

---

[30] See Section 2.2. above.

[31] Additionally, we have to assume that a new equilibrium with a common rate of profit in all sectors is reached instantaneously. Otherwise β would change into a vector which is itself independent of the price system. See Section 3.3. below.

of steady–state systems, then, Marx' second proposition on the rate of profit is clearly erroneous; while outside the steady state, it is undecidable, for in fact different economies are being compared.

3.2.4. Summary Remarks on Difference–Equation Models

In this section, we have reviewed several prominent difference–equation systems in economic theory with regard to their time consistency. Insofar as none of this models was originally presented in the literature as a difference–equation system, our choices may well seem to have been arbitrary. But unlike the systems discussed in Section 3.1., all the systems considered in this section could easily be reformulated in terms of the analysis of Chapter 2 without changing their assumptions or altering their results. In terms of these results, moreover, the systems of this sections can be interpreted so as to emphasize their close relationship to one another. Thus, if we isolate labor in the price equations of von Neumann's system and regard the material inputs to labor as consumption, we obtain the system of Sraffa. And if we isolate stocks of the durable means of production from the joint production processess of Sraffa, we obtain Marx' scheme of reproduction with a multiperiod turnover of capital goods, a representation at which Marx himself never arrived. Much of this is familiar, and perhaps well settled, at least as far as price systems are concerned. But when quantites and accumulation are considered, theoreticians of the Sraffa School would perhaps deny such a convergence, for accumulation schemes presuppose time and changing scales of activity. At pains to defend Sraffa's concept against charges of hidden assumptions regarding returns to scale, his followers insist that, to whatever extent they might be formally equivalent, there remain important differences between Sraffa's system and those of Marx and von Neumann[32]. Such problems apart, however, it is clear that both von Neumann's and Marx's systems perform with Sraffian prices.

One major change is observed when von Neumann's system is transformed so as to permit external consumption and external labor inputs: the generalized system no longer requires that the rate of output be equal to the rate of growth. This is most obvious in Sraffa's stationary state with positive interest, and it is equally true with growth. There is no strict duality between consumption and labor inputs, instead the money value of consumption may exceed or fall short of the money value of labor applied.

This observation proves useful in our discussion of the Marxian model as well. Since we require no optimization techniques to show the existence

---

[32] On Sraffa and Marx, see Steedman (1977); on Sraffa and von Neumann, see Schefold (1980).

This observation proves useful in our discussion of the Marxian model as well. Since we require no optimization techniques to show the existence of positive solutions, we obtain equilibria in which the rate of growth is not necessarily equal to the rate of interest. Employing the subsystem approach to the analysis of durable capital goods, the Marxian equations can be written in input–output notation without reference to the joint–production method. Nevertheless, it is clear that the basic lessons told by Sraffa's analysis still remain valid, for the change in value of a used capital good is determined by the value of its products, rather than being given as an exogenous side constraint before production commences.

Supplied with the reduced system in which capital goods have been aggregated away, we examine possible dynamic tendencies of the rate of profit. But it turns out that in the case of non–neutral technical progress, the structures of the economy at any given two points in time can scarcely be compared with one another. It thus seems impossible to make a clear prediction regarding the intertemporal behavior of the profit rate.

It has been seen that the Walrasian prices do not conform to the requirements of system theory, while, at least formally, Marxian prices do. But it is a well–known problem of Marxian theory that values and prices do not correspond to one another, which phenomenon is ordinarily termed the "Transformation Problem". We may thus reinterpret Walras' prices as values and examine their behavior along the lines of the discussion of the Marxian transformation problem.

3.3.   Conclusion (The Problem of Control II): The Generalized Transformation Problem of Value Theory

3.3.1.   Introduction

Not all of the theories we have considered so far are theories of value in the proper sense. von Neumann's theory, for example, offers a technical explanation of how prices emerge from prices and how interest intervenes between these two sets of prices, but no attempt is made to reduce prices to an external measure of value. To a certain extent, the same is true of Sraffa's theory, though scholars committed to the Sraffian point of view might well disagree. One the one hand, Sraffa assumes (contrary to von Neumann) that apart from produced commodities, the only source of value is unskilled labor, but on the other, he reckognizes that reducing prices to labor values is simply a limiting case of his own model. Sraffa makes extensive use of the aggregate of a standard commodity, but this is not itself an external source of value.

In addition to these systems, there are theories of value which ssek to determine relative prices in some way or another on the basis of external from the labor theory of value that a bias is introduced between relative values and relative prices by the different relations of direct to indirect labor embodied in unit prices; this is the "Transformation Problem". Here, I shall show the same transformation problem arises in the context of other theories of value as well; for time–consistent systems of production in general, the resultant price equations will, as a rule, yield relative prices that differ from the relative values predicted by the theory in question. In Section 3.3.2., we derive the transformation problem in general; the Marxian case is presented as an example in Section 3.3.3. We then turn in Section 3.3.4. to a demonstration that, when applied to time–consistent systems in the style of Section 3.1., the Walrasian value equations lead to a similar bias. The results of these sections suggest that, contrary to conventional wisdom of economic thought, economic activity can never be completely controlled by the system of prices, for that system is only incompletely controllable itself.

3.3.2. The Transformation Problem in General

Consider an array of external inputs $r_k, k = 1, \ldots, m$. Some of these will be free goods, others will be assigned positive values u_k. Because theories of value disagree as to which of these inputs do or do not carry positive values, we shall assume that the vector r of external inputs is strictly positive, while the vector of input values u is only nonnegative (though almost all theories of value claim that at least one element of u is in fact positive).

Obviously, a scale against which u can be measured is needed. Usually, some input m is taken as the basis of measurement, so all the $u_k, k < m$, reflect values per quantity unit of input m. Value theories of all kinds assume that produced commodities $i, i = 1, \ldots, n$ have their values as well, which we call v_i and which exist along with quantities x_i. The claim which is ordinarily made is that product values v_i can be reduced to input values u_k according to the input coefficients. In matrix notation, this is:

(3.3.1.) $$v' = v'A + u'D$$

It is clear that (3.3.1.) is the dual to the quantity system:

(3.3.2a.) $$x = Ax + Cx$$
(3.3.2b.) $$r = Dx$$

where time indices have been omitted. This will be demonstrated shortly. Taking the inverse in (3.3.2a.), we find:

(3.3.3.) $$x = (I - A)^{-1}Cx$$

145

We apply (3.3.2b.):

$$(3.3.4.) \qquad r = Dx = D(I - A)^{-1}Cx$$

so that the system–theoretic input–output form is found in which:

$$H \equiv D(I - A)^{-1}C$$

can be termed the state–transition matrix. By the same token, (3.3.1.) is:

$$(3.3.5.) \qquad v' = u'D(I - A)^{-1}$$

The values of consumer–good outputs are $v'C$, so:

$$(3.3.6.) \qquad v'C = u'D(I - A)^{-1}C$$

where once again the state–transition matrix is:

$$H \equiv D(I - A)^{-1}C$$

H is generally of full rank, for no column of either D or C is zero, A cannot be decomposed, and all matrices are semipositive. Given H of full rank, outputs can be completely controlled by prices; it is a familiar result in system theory that a completely controllable system can also be controlled by its dual. This property of controllability is the very essence of value theory. Markets act as mechanisms of control which reduce the economic problem to the choice between external instruments, that is, value–bearing inputs. If in the Walrasian world all agents are "rational" and choose among the alternatives available to them so as to maximize profits or utilty, prices will reflect the degree of scarcity and the allocation of outputs be such that a state of Pareto optimality is achieved; this, of course, is the task performed by the "Invisible Hand" of Adam Smith (1776)[33].

But there is a catch to all of this: we cannot be sure that markets operate with product values v_i as market prices, since time has been omitted from the calculations in equatins (3.3.1.) and (3.3.2). System theory, however, offers a tool for transforming a timeless system into a dynamic one. The

---

[33] Of course, this reasoning cannot be applied to the Marxist version of socialist theory, though it should be kept in mind that both Walras and Pareto were sympathetic with socialist ideas as well.

timeless equations can be understood as z–transforms of a dynamic system[34] such that, in our example:

(3.3.7a.) $$\tilde{x}_t = A\tilde{x}_{t+1} + C\tilde{x}_t$$

(3.3.7b.) $$\tilde{r}_t = D\tilde{x}_{t+1}$$

and, with respect to values:

(3.3.8.) $$\tilde{v}'_{t+1} = \tilde{v}'_t A + \tilde{u}'_t D$$

Equation (3.3.7.) is clearly the familiar backward–recursive system of quantities, while (3.3.8.) is a dynamical system of values which we have not encountered so far. Were these systems correctly to describe production and the formation of prices, all claims made by value theory would in fact be true. But there is a term missing in (3.3.8.), namely the (diagonal matrix of the) interest factor β. This factor intervenes between values and prices in a nontrivial way and is neither necessarily constant nor dependent upon inputs. It invariable arises as soon as dynamics are implied, a point which we have developed at length in the preceding chapters.

Consider the dynamic price system of Section 2.2.1.:

(3.3.9.) $$p'_{t+1} = \beta' \left(p'_t A + p'^{(r)}_t D \right)$$

which implies that inputs and preproducts must be paid at time t despite the fact that output is sold only at the later time $t + 1$. If time is discounted by the rate of interest, there will be an interest charge on circulating capital. A special case of (3.3.9.) is:

(3.3.10.) $$p'_t = \beta \left(p'_t A + p'^{(r)}_t D \right)$$

in which constant prices and uniform profits are assumed. The reduced form is then:

(3.3.11.) $$p'_t = p'^{(r)}_t D(\frac{1}{\beta} I - A)^{-1}$$

Applying the matrix of consumption ratios C, we have:

(3.3.12.) $$p'_t C = p'^{(r)}_t D(\frac{1}{\beta} I - A)^{-1} C$$

---

[34] See, for example, Luenberger (1979, Sec. 8.4.).

with the state–transition matrix:

$$(3.3.13.) \qquad \tilde{H} \equiv D(\frac{1}{\beta}I - A)^{-1}C$$

$\tilde{H}$ is not the same as H, and changes are wrought in p' and $\tilde{v}'$ as well, as (3.3.8.) and (3.3.10.) make clear. If we assume that input values are identical to input prices, $p'^{(r)}_t = \tilde{u}'$, rearrangement of terms yields:

$$(3.3.14.) \qquad \tilde{v}'(I - A) = p'(\frac{1}{\beta}I - A)$$

that is:

$$\tilde{v}'(I - A) = \frac{1 - \beta}{\beta}p' + \tilde{p}'(I - A)$$

$$(3.3.15.) \qquad v' = p'\left(I + \frac{1 - \beta}{\beta}(I - A)^{-1}\right)$$

This last equation shows that, as a rule, the vector of values is not a scalar multiple of the price vector, that is, the exchange rate between any two commodities expressed in terms of value is not equal to the exchange rate expressed in terms of prices.

This is the generalized transformation problem. It applies even if it is assumed that prices are constant over time and the rate of interest is uniform. Were it the case that the state–transition matrix $\tilde{H}$ of (3.3.13.) would apply also under dynamic conditions this would do no harm, for then the system could at least be controlled by these values. But on reintroducing dynamics we find the truly dynamical state transition matrix $\tilde{\tilde{H}}$ as:

$$(3.3.16.) \qquad \tilde{\tilde{H}} = D(\frac{1}{\beta'_t}I - A)^{-1}C$$

where now β' is again a vector. Now the rate of profit is neither uniform nor necessarily constant, there is no strict relation between values and prices as would be indicated by (3.3.12.). The behavior of prices therefore cannot be controlled by the prices of external inputs. Now since in a free market all outputs depend on prices we arrive at the conclusion that the behavior of input prices does not suffice to control the behavior of quantities produced. Therefore the economic self–regulation through labor values, scarcities etc. is impossible. This problem of control is the dynamic counterpart of the

Transformation Problem, and where the latter exists the former applies as well.

3.3.3.   The Marxian Transformation Problem

The transformation problem is a central feature of the standard critique of Marxian economic doctrine[35]. What follows is a summary of the results presented in such work as that of Okishio (1963). Let human labor be the sole external input to production, with l' as its input vector[36]. As before, let v' be the vector of values and A be the technical input–output matrix, which the value of human labor equal to unity. The labor theory of value holds that all values are given by the sum of direct labor values and the indirect values of dated labor:

(3.3.17.) $$v' = v'A + l'$$

from which:

(3.3.18.) $$v' = (I - A)^{-1}l'$$

Under the conditions of capitalism, interest on circulating capital is charged. Thus, the price equation is:

(3.3.19.) $$p' = \beta(p'A + wl')$$

where w is the wage rate for unskilled labour. Normalizing, we find:

(3.3.20.) $$p'^+ \equiv \frac{1}{w}p' = (\frac{1}{\beta}I - A)^{-1}l'$$

By analogy to (3.3.14.), we have:

(3.3.21.) $$v'(I - A) = p'^+(\frac{1}{\beta}I - A)$$

and (3.3.15.) applies once more:

$$v' = p'^+ \left(I + \frac{1-\beta}{\beta}(I - A)^{-1}\right)$$

---

[35] An early formal elaboration is von Bortkiewicz (1906, 1907), a review of the discussion is included also in Engels' preface to the third (1894) volume of "Capital".

[36] There clearly must be inputs of raw materials as well, but sine they bear no embodied labor values, these are not traded commodities.

This is the original Marxist version of the Transformation Problem. The rate of exchange between any two commodities expressed in terms of prices is in general not equal to the exchange rate expressed in terms of labor values. It is ironic that Marxian doctrine has been criticized for this inconsistency by theorists in the Walrasian tradition[37], for in fact the Walrasian system itself suffers from much the same deficiency.

3.3.4. The Walrasian Transformation Problem

We now turn to Walrasian values. There are k distinct (external) scarce inputs, whose input quantities form a vector r and, similarly, n distinct scarce outputs which form a vector x. The spaces spanned by these vectors may be identical, and the difference between these vectors themselves is, in terms of activity analysis, equal to the "netput" vector (see Koopmans (1951)). To each input resource is assigned a price vector u', while commodity prices are denoted by the vector v' (both vectors may be identical in the netput case). Once again, let A be the technical input–output matrix of intermediate commodities and D be the technical input–output matrix of external inputs. Recalling the analysis of Section 3.1.2. above and replacing $p'^{(r)}$ by u' and $p'^{(x)}$ by v', we may express the Walrasian price system as:

$$(3.3.22.) \qquad\qquad v' = v'A + u'D$$

Assuming equilibrium, market prices are given by:

$$(3.3.23.) \qquad\qquad p' = \beta(p'A + p'^{(r)}D)$$

and, using (3.3.14.), we find once more that:

$$v' = p'\left(I + \frac{1-\beta}{\beta}(I-A)^{-1}\right)$$

This is the Walrasian transformation problem. It is apparently a generalization of the problem which arises in Marxian theory, with the vector of labor–input coefficients replaced by a more inclusive matrix of resource–input coefficients. A moment's thought makes clear why these two systems, despite the vast difference in the intentions of their authors, are so very similar in their most telling weaknesses. In "capitalist" economies, the rate of interest is simply a price at which assets of different maturity are traded against

---

[37] See, for example, Samuelson (1957, 1971).

one another. But in its reduction of values to labor inputs, Marxian value theory rejects such discounting, and in fact identifies it as the major source of exploitation in capitalist economies. In this way, the element of time is implicitly removed from the analysis of value. Walrasian theory, on the other hand, is concerned with the conditions under which equilibrium will exist for every economic agent and thus for the economy as a whole. At first glance, this appears to be the case whenever the value of the resources held by any individual is equal to the value of the goods which might eventually be produced from them. It then makes no difference which of these forms of wealth are held as a medium of exchange, and the problem of production reduces to the problem of exchange. In order to work out these conditions most clearly, Walras explicitly ignores the element of time, and in doing so assumes the existence of interest away. But real market processes take time, and as time is introduced into Walras' world, a transformation problem arises.

Both theories share a common view with regard to the problem of control: if the economy were such that the laws of value promulgated by these systems were obeyed, no distortion of the economic process could arise. Thus, the claim of both value theories is that economic malfunction is the result of exogenous causes, be it capitalists' fetishism of accumulation identified by Marxits or the Walrasian bogey of less than perfect competition in the formation of prices. The transformation problem, however, suggests that such reasoning is highly misleading, for the (self–) control of economic performance by values is impossible as long as the rate of interest exists to provide a degree of freedom in the system[38].

In conclusion, we find that the contribution of traditional price theory to the understanding of price formation must not be overestimated. Sraffa (1960) has argued for the impossibility to determine relative prices through exogenous values in a stationary–state setting. A system–theoretic view supports this result and offers a dynamic interpretation for it: since the rate of interest cannot be determined within the economic system, it is impossible for the system of prices to completely control the allocation of economic

---

[38] It is interesting to note that in his defense of the aggregate production function, Samuelson (1962) employs the assumption that the proportion of direct to indirect resource values is identical in all production lines, that is, that the organic composition of capital is equal in all industries. This implies that an aggregate production function and a unique wage–interest frontier exist if the transformation problem is neglected. The Cambridge Controversy has shown that the converse holds true as well. Given an economy with circulating capital, it is impossible to determine the rate of interest as a well–behaved function of the technique of production.

goods, even if we neglect the fact that equilibrium theory might itself be an inadequate tool for such dynamic analysis. But system theory calls for models which can be meaningfully interpreted even outside the steady–state equilibrium. None of the economic theories examined here comprises such a system, for they are constrained to the assumption (as opposed to the proof) that markets will clear. A truly dynamical theory of prices would have to explain what happens to prices, quantities and profits in the state of disequilibrium. Yet there seems to be no unambiguous strategy for designing such theories which does not entail restrictive and possibly *ad hoc* behavioral assumptions. Economic theory is on firm ground only where the physical relations of quantities are examined. The rest depends on historical patterns of scientific judgement and perspective, and it is precisely here that the unavoidable "softness" of economic science is most clearly revealed.

Bibliography

AOKI, M. (1976): *Optimal Control and System Theory in Dynamic Economic Analysis*. New York: North Holland.

ARROW, K. (1964): "Optimal Capital Policy, the Cost of Capital, and Myopic Decision Rules", *Annals of the Institute of Statistical Mathematics*, 16, 21–30.

— / L. HURWICZ (1958): "On the Stability of the Competitive Equilibrium I", *Econometrica*, 26, 522–552.

— / D. STARRETT (1971): "Cost– and Demand–Theoretic Approaches to the Theory of Prices", in: *Carl Menger and the Austrian School of Economics*, ed. by J.R. Hicks and W. Weber, Oxford: Clarendon Press.

BAUMOL, W. (1947): *Economic Dynamics*, New York: Macmillan.

BECKMANN, M. (1971): "The Period of Production in a von Neumann World", in: *Contributions to the von Neumann Model*, ed. by G. Bruckmann and W. Weber, Vienna: Springer.

BLATT, J.M. (1983): *Dynamic Economic Systems*, New York: Sharpe.

BLISS, C.D. (1977): *Capital Theory and the Distribution of Income*, Amsterdam: North Holland.

BÖHM–BAWERK, E. von (1959 (1884)): *Capital and Interest Vol. 1: The History and Critique of Interest Theories*, South Holland, Ill.: Libertarian Press.

— (1959 (1889)): *Capital and Interest Vol. 2: Positive Theory of Capital*, South Holland, Ill.: Libertarian Press.

BORTKIEWICZ, L. von (1906): "Wertrechnung und Preisrechnung im Marxschen System I", *Archiv für Sozialwissenschaft und Sozialpolitik*, 23, 1–50.

— (1907): "Wertrechnung und Preisrechnung im Marxschen System II", *Archiv für Sozialwissenschaft und Sozialpolitik*, 25, 10–51.

BURMEISTER, E. (1974): "Synthesizing the Neo–Austrian and Alternative Approaches to Capital Theory", *Journal of Economic Literature*, 12, 413–456.

— (1980): *Capital Theory and Dynamics*, Cambridge: Cambridge University Press.

— / E. SHESHINSKI (1968): "A Nonsubstitution Theorem in a Model With Fixed Capital", *Southern Economic Journal*, 35, 273–276.

— / R. DOBELL (1970): *Mathematical Theories of Economic Growth*, London: Macmillan.

CASSEL, G. (1923 (1918)): *Theory of the Social Economy*, London: T.F. Unwin.

CASTI, J. (1977): *Dynamical Systems and Their Applications*, New York: Academic Press.

CHIPMAN, J.S. (1950): "The Multi–Sector Multiplier", *Econometrica*, 18, 355–374.

CHRISTENSEN, L.R. / D.W. JORGENSON (1973): "Measuring the Performance of the Private Sector of the U.S. Economy, 1929–1969", in: *Measuring Social and Economic Performance*, ed. by M. Moss, New York: National Bureau of Economic Research.

CLARK, J.B. (1888): *Capital and Its Earnings*, Baltimore: American Economic Association.

— (1899): *The Distribution of Wealth*, New York: Macmillan.

COLLATZ, L. (1949): *Eigenwertaufgaben mit technischen Anwendungen*, Leipzig: Akademische Verlagsgesellschaft Geest & Portig.

DEBREU, G. (1959): *Theory of Value*, New York: Wiley.

DORFMAN, R./P.A. SAMUELSON/R.M. SOLOW (1958): *Linear Programming and Economic Analysis*, New York: McGraw–Hill.

DUCHIN, F. / D.B. SZYLD (1985) "A Dynamic Input–Output–Model with Assured Positive Output" *Metroeconomica*, 37, 269–282.

EATWELL, J. (1975) *Scarce and Produced Commodities: An Examination of Some Fundamentals in the Theory of Value, with Particular Reference to the Works of Ricardo and Walras*, Dissertation, Harvard University.

EUCKEN, W. (1926): *Kapitaltheoretische Untersuchungen*, Jena: Fischer.

FABER, M. (1979): *Introduction to Modern Austrian Capital Theory*, Berlin: Springer.

FISHER I. (1930): *The Theory of Interest*, New York: Macmillan.

FRISCH, R. (1935/36): "On the Notion of Equilibrium and Disequilibrium", *Review of Economic Studies*, 3, 100-106.

FUJIMOTO, T. (1983): "Duality in Capital Theory with Variable Consumption: A Comment", *Zeitschrift für Nationalökonomie*, 43, 213–217.

GAREGNANI, P. (1976): "On a Change in the Notion of Equilibrium in Recent Work on Value and Distribution", in: *Essays in Modern Capital Theory*, ed. by M. Brown, K. Sato and P. Zarembka, Amsterdam: North Holland.

GEORGESCU–ROEGEN, N. (1966): "Some Orientation Issues in Economics", in: N. Georgescu–Roegen: *Analytical Economic Issues and Problems*, Cambridge, Mass.: Harvard University Press.

— (1971): *The Entropy Law and the Economic Process*, Cambrige, Mass.: Harvard University Press.

GOODWIN, R.M. (1947): "Dynamical Coupling with Especial Reference to Markets Having Production Lags", *Econometrica*, 18 (1947), 355–374.

HAHN, F. (1982): "The Neo–Ricardians", *Cambridge Journal of Economics*, 6, 353–374.

HALL, R.E. (1968): "Technical Change and Capital from the Point of the Dual", *Review of Economic Studies* 35, 35–46.

HAUSMAN, D.M. (1981): *Capital, Profits, and Prices*, New York: Columbia University Press.

HAWKINS, D./H.A. SIMON (1948): "Some Conditions of Macroeconomic Stability", *Econometrica*, 17, 245–248.

HAYEK, F.A. von (1931): *Prices and Production*, London: Routlegde & Kegan Paul.

— (1941): *The Pure Theory of Capital*, London: Macmillan.

HICKS, J.R. (1941): *Value and Capital*, Oxford: Clarendon Press.

— (1965): *Capital and Growth*, Oxford: Clarendon Press.

— (1973): *Capital and Time*, Oxford: Clarendon Press.

HOTELLING, H.S. (1925): "A General Mathematical Theory of Depreciation", *Journal of the American Statistical Association* 20, 340–353.

— (1931): "The Economics of Exhaustible Resources", *Journal of Political Economy*, 39, 137–175.

JAKSCH, H.J. (1975): *Theorie linearer Wirtschaftsmodelle*, Vol. 2, Tübingen: Mohr (Siebeck).

JOHANSEN, L. (1978): "On the Theory of Dynamic Input–Output Models with Different Time Profiles of Capital Construction and Finite Lifetime of Capital Equipment", *Journal of Economic Theory*, 19, 513–541.

JORGENSON, D.W. (1960): "On a Dual Stability Theorem", *Econometrica*, 28, 892–899.

— (1961): "Stability of a Dynamic Input–Output System", *Review of Economic Studies*, 28, 105–116.

— (1973): "The Economic Theory of Replacement and Depreciation", in: *Econometrics and Economic Theory, Essays in Honour of Jan Tinbergen*, ed. by W. Sellekaerts, New York: Macmillan.

— (1980): "Accounting for Capital", in: *Capital, Efficiency and Growth*, ed. by G.M. von Furstenberg, Cambridge, Mass.: Ballinger.

KALMAN, R.E. (1980): "System–Theoretic Critique of Dynamic Economic Models", *International Journal of Policy Analysis and Information Systems*, 4, 3–22.

— (1982): "Dynamic Econometric Models: A System–Theoretic Critique", in: *New Quantitative Techniques for Economic Analysis*, ed. by G.P. Szegö, New York: Academic Press.

— /P.L. FALB/M.A. ARBIB (1968): *Topics in Mathematical System Theory*, New York: McGraw–Hill.

KEMENY, J.G./O. MORGENSTERN/G.L. THOMPSON (1956): "A Generalization of the von Neumann Model of an Expanding Economy", *Econometrica*, 24, 115–135.

KEYFITZ, N. (1968): *Introduction to the Mathematics of Populations*, Reading, Mass: Addison–Wesley.

KNAPP, G.F. (1868): *Über die Ermittlung der Sterblichkeit aus den Aufzeichnungen der Be völkerungsstatistik*, Leipzig: Hinrich.

KOOPMANS, T.C. (ed.) (1951): *Activity Analysis of Production and Allocation*, New York: Wiley.

LEONTIEF, W.W. (1928): "Die Wirtschaft als Kreislauf", *Archiv für Sozialwissenschaft und Sozialpolitik*, 60, 577–623.

— (1941): *The Structure of the American Economy 1919–1939*, New York: Macmillan.

— (1951): *The Structure of the American Economy 1919–1939*, 2nd ed. New York: Oxford University Press.

— et al. (1953): *Studies in the Structure of the American Economy*. New York: Oxford University Press.

LEXIS, W. (1874): *Einleitung in die Theorie der Bevölkerungsstatistik*, Straßburg: Trübner.

LIVESEY, D.A. (1973): "The Singularity Problem in the Dynamic Input–Output Model", *International Journal of Systems Science*, 4, 437–440.

LÖWE, A. (1926): "Wie ist Konjunkturtheorie überhaupt möglich?", *Weltwirtschaftliches Archiv*, 24, 165–197.

LOTKA, A. (1939): *Théorie analytique des associations biologiques, P. II: Analyse démographique avec application particulière à l' espèce humaine*, Paris: Hermann.

LUENBERGER, D.G. (1979): *Introduction to Dynamic Systems*, New York: Wiley.

LUTZ, F.A. (1967 (1954)): *The Theory of Interest*, Dordrecht: Reidel.

MAINWARING, L. (1982): "Duality in Capital Theory with variable Consumption: A Note", *Zeitschrift für Nationalökonomie*, 42, 87–90.

MALINVAUD, E. (1953): "Capital Accumulation and Efficient Allocation of Resources", *Econometrica*, 21, 233–268.

MARX, K. (1968 (1849)): "Wage Labor and Capital", in: *Karl Marx and Frederick Engels, Selected Works*, London: Lawrence & Wishart.

— (1970 (1859)): *Zur Kritik der politischen Ökonomie*, Berlin: Duncker & Humblot. Tansl. as: *Contributions to the Critique of Political Economy*, London: Lawrence & Wishart.

— (1978 (1885)): *Capital* Vol. II, Hammondsworth: Penguin Books.

— (1981 (1894)): *Capital* Vol. III, Hammondsworth: Penguin Books.

MENGER, C. (1981 (1871)): *Grundsätze der Volkswirtschaftslehre*, transl. as: *Principles of Economics*, New York: New York University Press.

METZLER, L.A. (1950): "A Multiple–Region Theory of Income and Trade", *Econometrica*, 18, 329–354.

MILL, J.St. (1848): *Principles of Political Economy*, Collected Works, Toronto: Toronto University Press.

MORGENSTERN, O./G.L. THOMPSON (1967): "Private and Public Consumption and Savings in the von Neumann Model of an Expanding Economy", *Kyklos*, 20, 387–409.

MORISHIMA, M. (1958): "Prices, Interest, and Profits in a Dynamic Leontief Model", *Econometrica*, 26, 358–380.

— (1964): *Equilibrium, Stability, and Growth*, Oxford: Clarendon Press.

— (1973): *Marx's Economics*, Cambridge: Cambridge University Press.

— (1977): *Walras' Economics*, Cambridge: Cambridge University Press.

—/G. CATEPHORES (1978): *Value, Exploitation and Growth*, London: McGraw–Hill.

NELSON, R.R./S.G. WINTER (1982): *An Evolutionary Theory of Economic Change*, Cambridge, Mass.: Harvard University Press.

NEUMANN, J. von (1945 (1937)): "A Model of General Economic Equilibrium", *Review of Economic Studies*, 13, 1–9.

NIKAIDÔ, H. (1962): "Some Dynamic Phenomena in the Dynamic Leontief Model of the Reversely Lagged Type", *Review of Economic Studies*, 29, 313–323.

— (1968): *Convex Structures and Economic Theory*, New York: Academic Press.

OKISHIO, N. (1963): "A Mathematical Note on Marxian Theorems", *Weltwirtschaftliches Archiv*, 91, 287–299.

OROSEL, G. (1977): *Ungleichschrittiges Wachstum bei linearer Technologie*, Berlin: Duncker & Humblot.

— (1979): "A Reformulation of the Austrian Theory of Capital and Its Application to Reswitching and Related Phenomena", *Zeitschrift für Nationalökonomie*, 39, 1–31.

— (1981): "Faber's Modern Austrian Capital Theory: A Critique", *Zeitschrift für Nationalökonomie*, 41, 141–155.

PASINETTI, L. (1977): *Lectures on the Theory of Production*, New York: Columbia University Press.

— (1980): "A Note on Basics, Non–Basics, and Joint Production", in: *Essays on the Theory of Joint Production*, ed. by L. Pasinetti, New York: Columbia University Press.

REISS, W. (1981): *Umwegproduktion und Positivität des Zinses*, Berlin: Duncker & Humblot.

RICARDO, D. (1951 (1817)): *Principles of Political Economy and Taxation, The Works and Correspondence of David Ricardo* Vol. I, ed. by P. Sraffa and M. Dobb, Cambridge: Cambridge University Press.

RITSCHL, A. (1988): "Dynamic Systems and Input–Output Theory", in: *Recent Approaches to Economic Dynamics*, ed. by P. Flaschel and M. Krüger, Frankfurt: Lang, forthcoming.

ROBINSON, J. (1938): "The Classification of Inventions", *Review of Economic Studies*, 5, 139–142.

— (1942): *An Essay in Marxian Economics*, London: Macmillan.

— (1954): "The Production Function and the Theory of Capital", *Review of Economic Studies*, 21, 81–106.

ROCKAFELLAR, R.T. (1974): "Convex Algebra and Duality in Dynamic Models of Production", in: *Mathematical Models in Economics*, Amsterdam: North Holland.

RODBERTUS–JAGETZOW, K. von (1851): *Soziale Briefe an v. Kirchmann, Dritter Brief*, Berlin: Puttkamer & Mühlbrecht.

ROEMER, J. (1981): *Analytical Foundations of Marxian Economic Theory*, Cambridge: Cambridge University Press.

RONCAGLIA, A. (1978): *Sraffa and the Theory of Prices*, Chichester: Wiley.

SAMUELSON, P.A. (1947): *Foundations of Economic Analysis*, Cambridge, Mass.: Harvard University Press.

— (1957): "Wages and Interest: A Modern Dissection of Marxian Economic Models", *American Economic Review*, 47, 884–912.

— (1962): "Parable and Realism in Capital Theory: The Surrogate Production Function", *Review of Economic Studies*, 28, 193–207.

— (1971): "Understanding the Marxian Notion of Exploitation", *Journal of Economic Literature*, 9, 399–431.

— (1983): "von Thünen at Two Hundred", *Journal of Economic Literature* 21, 1448–1488.

SCHEFOLD, B. (1977): "Fixed Capital as a Joint Product and the Analysis of Accumulation With Different Forms of Technical Progress", in: *Essays on the Theory of Joint Production*, ed. by L. Pasinetti, New York: Columbia University Press.

— (1980): "von Neumann and Sraffa: Mathematical Equivalence and Conceptual Difference", *Economic Journal*, 90, 140–156.

SHACKLE, G.L. (1958): *Time in Economics*, Amsterdam: North Holland.

SOLOW, R.M. (1952): "On the Structure of Linear Models", *Econometrica*, 21, 29–46.

— (1959): "Competitive Valuation in a Dynamic Input–Output Model", *Econometrica*, 27, 30–53.

—/P.A. SAMUELSON (1953): "Balanced Growth Under Constant Returns to Scale", *Econometrica*, 21, 412–424.

— et al. (1966): "Neoclassical Growth With Fixed Factor Proportions", *Review of Economic Studies*, 33, 79–116.

SRAFFA, P. (1960): *Production of Commodities by Means of Commodities*, Cambridge: Cambridge University Press.

STEEDMAN, I. (1976): "Positive Profits with Negative Surplus Values", *Economic Journal*, 86, 114–123.

— (1977): *Marx After Sraffa*, London: New Left Books.

SWEEZY, P. (1952): *The Theory of Capitalist Development*, London: Dennis Dobson.

VAHRENKAMP, R. (1977): *Kegelbalanciertes Wachstum*, Meisenheim: Athenäum/Hain.

WALRAS, L. (1954 (1871, 1877, 1926)): *Elements of Pure Economics*, London: Allen & Unwin.

WAN, H.Y. jr. (1971): *Economic Growth*, New York: Harcourt, Brace, Jovanovich.

WEIZSÄCKER, C.C. von (1971): *Steady–State Capital Theory*, Berlin: Springer.

WICKSELL, K. (1934 (1913)): *Lectures on Political Economy*, London: Routledge & Kegan Paul.

WIELANDT, H. (1950): "Unzerlegbare nichtnegative Matrizen", *Mathematische Zeitschrift*, 642–648.